WHEN ADAM DELVED AND EVE SPAN

History and politics titles from New Clarion Press

Lawrence Black et al., *Consensus or Coercion? The State, the People and Social Cohesion in Post-war Britain*

John Carter and Dave Morland (eds), *Anti-Capitalist Britain*

Keith Flett and David Renton (eds), *New Approaches to Socialist History*

Duncan Hall, *'A Pleasant Change from Politics': Music and the British Labour Movement between the Wars*

Anne Kerr and Tom Shakespeare, *Genetic Politics: From Eugenics to Genome*

Mark O'Brien, *When Adam Delved and Eve Span: A History of the Peasants' Revolt of 1381*

David Renton, *Classical Marxism: Socialist Theory and the Second International*

David Stack, *The First Darwinian Left: Socialism and Darwinism 1859–1914*

Leo Zeilig (ed.), *Class Struggle and Resistance in Africa*

WHEN ADAM DELVED AND EVE SPAN

A HISTORY OF THE PEASANTS' REVOLT OF 1381

Mark O'Brien

New Clarion Press

First published 2004

New Clarion Press
5 Church Row, Gretton
Cheltenham GL54 5HG
England

New Clarion Press is a workers' co-operative.

A catalogue record for this book is available from the British Library.

ISBN   1 873797 45 1

Typeset in Perpetua by Jean Wilson Typesetting, Coventry
Printed in Great Britain by The Cromwell Press, Trowbridge

For Kate and Rohina

✠

Dedicated to all who rebel

When Adam delved and Eve span,
Who was then a gentleman?

A fourteenth-century rhyme

CONTENTS

PREFACE

The aim of this book is a modest one. It is to tell the story of one of the most extraordinary episodes in English history in a manner that is, hopefully, accessible, exciting and enjoyable to the reader. It does not offer new research drawn from recently discovered primary sources or anything of the like. Nor does it offer original analytical frameworks or perspectives. Indeed, the reliance on the work of others will be obvious and acknowledged throughout.

It is also beyond the scope of this book – as well as the competence of the author – to assess the accounts given in the early chronicles. As is well known amongst scholars of the period, the chronicles do not agree on some important details – the role of John Ball, the precise sequence of events on 13 June 1381, the location of the king at various points and so on. However, the general consensus given in the most authoritative histories has been taken at face value and presented in this historical introduction.

What is offered here is an account that is overwhelmingly sympathetic to the key actors in this unique historical drama – the peasants of late-fourteenth-century England. For what it is worth, also, it is an account told by someone who, on discovering the story for himself, was amazed and inspired. It is this sense of inspiration, and the desire to share the story with a wider audience, that has motivated the writing of this short book.

Mark O'Brien
Liverpool, 2004

CHAPTER 1

THE MEDIEVAL SCENE

Not seldom I please myself with trying to realize the face of medieval England; the many chases and great woods, the great stretches of common village and common pasture quite unenclosed; the rough husbandry of the tilled parts, the unimproved breeds of cattle, sheep and swine, especially the latter, so lank and long and lathy, looking so strange to us; the strings of packhorses along the bridle roads; the scantiness of the wheel roads, scarce any except those left by the Romans, and those made from monastery to monastery; the scarcity of bridges, and people using ferries instead, or fords where they could; the little towns well bechurched, often walled; the villages just where they are now (except for those that have nothing left but the church to tell of them), but better and more populous; their churches, some big and handsome, some small and curious, but all crowded with altars and furniture, and gay with pictures and ornament; the many religious houses with their glorious architecture; the beautiful manor houses, some of them castles once, and survivals from an earlier period; some new and elegant; some out of all proportion small for the importance of their lords.[1]

In this passage William Morris knowingly idealizes the medieval world by way of contrast with the ugliness of the industrial towns of his own day. The scenic vista of feudal times in the eye of Morris's imagination of course disguises the grim realities of life for most people of the time. This passage, however, evokes something of the way things must have looked. With most of the country covered by wood and fen, this was indeed a more natural, a more nature-dominated, world than our own. The air the people breathed was clean and the water they drank was uncontaminated by chemical and human waste. But equally the diseases they contracted were debilitating, regular and frequently fatal. This was

1

an age of fears. Fears of the wildness of the woodlands, of the vagaries of climate, of the failure of harvest and of the dangers of childbirth. When times were good, when the harvest was successful, there could also be drunkenness, celebration and merriment within closed and strong village communities.

In our period, the mid to late fourteenth century, 95 per cent of the population was rural. People lived in small, scattered village communities that were sometimes located far from other settlements and were almost autonomous of their neighbours. They worked the *severalty* of small parcels of land divided amongst themselves. Increasingly, however, the villages clustered together, either near to, or certainly in the economic and social orbit of, one of the great manor houses of a region. Less often they would be located right alongside a manor house and its land or *demesne*. The boundaries of the *vill* might even enclose the manor house if they were large enough.

The life of the village was, compared to our own experience, claustrophobic and rule-bound. More often than not, these were exclusive communities with very clear demarcations as to who was and who was not a member of the village. A baker, for example, who was discovered to be withholding stock to raise the price, or a brewer who watered down their ale, could be expelled from the village. This was an age where standardization and issues of ownership and legal status were not as clearly defined as they were to become with the rise of capitalism, and squabbles between neighbours were constant. These were settled through the raising of the 'hue and cry' and the court of the manor. The range of 'hue and cry' disputes gives us an insight into what daily life in the village must have been like. Disputes arose over fences between holdings, over the trampling of crops by a neighbour's animals, over the bartering of goods, over theft, over slander and over matters of family and personal life. Violence within the village was common, and murder was not an infrequent means of settling disputes.[2]

The material aspect of the lives of these people was crude. The clothes they wore were made of rough woollen worsteds. The houses were of timber, the quality of the construction and materials varying somewhat from region to region and in terms of the specific circumstances of the family. A stone building, such as a granary, might exist here and there.[3] The food of the peasants was, by our own standards, monotonous and short on protein. Bacon and mutton were staple meats if the family was fortunate. Common vegetables were cabbages, leeks and pulses. Eggs and cheese provided some variety. The bread was made of barley.[4] The peasants fared a little better when the harvest had to be brought in and the lord might be persuaded to show some pragmatic generosity. The picture we are given is one of 'harvest workers and their dependants of the thirteenth century sitting down to heavy meals of barley bread and cheese, accompanied by a little salt meat or preserved fish, with ale, milk and water to drink'.[5]

The manor, around which the medieval village revolved, was a highly organized economic unit. At the head of the manor were, of course, the lord and his family. But on a large manor several layers of administration might exist for the daily running of things. The most entrusted and powerful of the manorial administrators would be the *seneschal*, who would have full knowledge of all of the holdings and activities of the manorial estate. Work discipline on the lord's demesne was the special responsibility of the *bailiff*, who kept a sharp eye out for shirking or dodging of dues and rents. Enforcing punishments for such defaults was also the job of the bailiff. Beneath the bailiff was the *reeve*. The reeve took practical responsibility for such daily tasks as the feeding and tethering of livestock and general animal husbandry. Other specialized occupations included the plough driver, the baker, the shepherd, the carter, the dairymaid, the hayward, the carpenter and the potter – though some of these latter trades might be provided by surrounding villages.[6] Of all of these, however:

> The most important was the smith working in iron; he made or repaired the iron parts of ploughs or carts, shoed horses and oxen, made or sharpened sickles, scythes, axes and knives, and provided hooks and nails for buildings. The ironsmith's forge was a focus of village life, and over and above this, the mysteries of his craft gave him an almost magical prestige.[7]

At the bottom of this social pyramid was the peasant, for whom the central fact of life was back-breaking, arduous and unremitting labour. And this was the great difference between the life of the manor and the life of the village. Far from the royal court, the

The unfree villeins led lives of back-breaking toil under the rod of the bailiff.

material surroundings of a local lord as well as his diet and material comforts were sometimes not so vastly different from those of his workers – except in quantity. But the lord and his family did not work. The freedom of the lord, of course, depended upon the unfreedom of the peasant – upon exploitation. The bonded serf and his family were required to pay rent for the land that they worked. The form of this rent varied from place to place and at different times of the year. There would be food to be given up in the form of food tribute. A proportion of the harvest was always handed over. More commonly, there was rent to be paid in the form of labour and services rendered to the lord's demesne. Increasingly by the fourteenth century there were money rents to be paid, such as the *tallage* – an annual rent paid by all peasants on the lord's estate. The lord took and the peasant paid.

The lives of the peasants were dominated by work. In between the harvests, the men would be turning over new land, digging ditches and weeding, and the land had to be cleared and ploughed. Women were found in the fields during the harvest. At other times they were cultivating the family croft to add fruit, vegetables and eggs to the family diet. They were spinning flax and dairying. They were mending garments and sacks. The work of the peasant family was repetitive and cyclic, as it rotated around planting and harvesting the crop. If the peasant was able, he would put some labour into the piece of land put aside for his own subsistence and that of his family. The harsh reality was, however, that a full half of peasant families lived constantly on the edge of hunger.[8]

The legal position of peasants and their families fell broadly into two types: the free peasants and the unfree peasants. The free peasantry lived hard lives but they were less legally and materially oppressed. They worked on their own plots of land, the *allods*, and were not beholden to any particular lord. They paid taxes only to the Church and the monarch and, to protect their legal status, they had access to the royal court. Whether a family was free or not was largely a matter of historical accident, and disputes by a family over their status occurred frequently in the manorial and royal courts. But our greatest sympathy must go to the peasants who were unfree – the serfs or *villeins*.

The situation of the villeins was truly miserable. The essential primary producers of the feudal system, they were accorded a social status barely above that of the animal world. The Franciscan, Alvarus Pelagius, writing near the beginning of the fourteenth century, made his opinion of the lives of the peasants clear:

> *For even as they plough and dig the earth all day long, so they become altogether earthy; they lick the earth, they eat the earth, they speak of earth; in the earth they have reposed all their hopes, nor do they care a jot for the heavenly substance that shall remain.*[9]

The lord had legal control and possession of every aspect of the villein's life. It was said of the villeins that they possessed 'nothing but their bellies'.[10] In England the villeins had no right of migration. This contrasted with their French counterparts, who had the right to leave the estate on the condition that they relinquished all possessions. In England villeins were bonded with the land and were treated as being inseparable from it in law. There were no common rights in the sense that we understand today. Under feudalism the peasant family and the individuals within it were regarded only in their economic aspect, in terms of their productive value.

*His progeny were not called familia in legal documents, but
sequela — 'brood' or 'litter'. Again, since this little holding
was not legally his own, and he was only a life tenant, therefore
the lord took a fine to himself at every change of tenancy. At the
serf's death . . . the lord could claim his best beast under the
name of 'heriot'; and in many cases the priest took the second
beast as a 'mortuary'. If he died with less than three beasts, the
best domestic possession could be claimed; a brass pot, for
instance, or a cloak . . . Again, just as the serf was not permitted
to leave the land, so neither was his offspring. If a girl married
without leave, the father was fined; and in some cases a fine was
taken even for marriage by permission. Still more odious and
unpopular than the heriot was the 'merchet', or fine taken for a
girl's marriage off the manor. By such marriages the lord lost
the hope of her brood, and must therefore be indemnified in
money . . . For the bondsman's whole position was such as to put
economic questions in the foreground; therefore widows, like
unmarried girls, were often treated as chattels. They were fined
for marrying without the lord's leave; or again, they might be
compelled to marry at his will, when he felt that the holding
was being neglected for the lack of a strong labourer's arm. It
may be that this did not happen very often; but certainly it was
frequent enough everywhere to mark a strong distinction
between medieval and modern society.[11]*

Feudalism may have treated the peasant as an animal. But the
peasants, of course, were not animals and they needed more than
fines and the bailiff's rod to keep them in their place. The medieval
world was an ideological world and on a daily basis the priest played
a much more central role than the soldier in maintaining the social
order. By the beginning of the fourteenth century, England had
around 9,000 parishes for a population of four and a half million.
Each parish, then, possessed about 450 parishioners – perhaps 180
adults. Altogether there were probably something like 20,000
priests.[12] The Christian Church reached deep and capillary like into
the social body of the medieval world. Through tithes and rents,
masses, blessings and sacraments, from the pulpit and through the
confessional, it encompassed the life experience of the peasant. Its
constant and pervasive presence was felt socially, economically and

mentally. In many ways this is where the peasant might feel their oppression the most.

In the realm of religion we see exploitation intersect with belief. There is no question that the Church bore heavily down, in the most directly material sense, upon the life of the peasant. Frequently, by the late medieval period Church institutions might be the largest owners of serfs in a particular region. When Pope Gregory liberated two serfs from bondage, it was commonly said that the lofty rhetoric which accompanied the act betrayed a guilty conscience. The Papal estates were based on the labour of thousands of serfs and theological orthodoxy taught that hereditary serfdom was justified by the sins of the parents. But the clergy exploited all peasants. The priest took 10 per cent of all peasant income. But this was not the end of the matter. The peasant family would periodically also have to pay 'great tithes' on crops and cattle as well as 'lesser tithes' on everything else produced by the peasant and his family. These included tithes of wool, flax, pot-herbs, leeks, apples, cheese, butter, milk, eggs, calves, chickens, geese, hens, sucking pigs, bees and honey as well as the produce of the craftsmen of the village. A 'tithe' would be two-thirds of the peasant's holdings, an 'offering' one-fifth and a 'glebe' one-eighth. The village priest could also act on behalf of the lord. Through the power of the confessional, the priest ensured that tithes were paid and that the peasant did not work 'fervently before [the lord's] face, but feebly and remissly behind his back'. It was not unusual for penance to include the payment of goods to the lord or to the archbishop. And yet the economic aspect of the relationship between the peasant and the Church was only one part of what was happening in society.

By the late Middle Ages, people had long grouped themselves into 'those who work, those who fight and those who pray'. There was a sense of reciprocity. Whereas the lord exploited his peasants, he was also expected to provide protection against thieves and brigands, and to administer justice in the village. Similarly, the Church was expected to provide a moral authority, a just fear of the Lord, reassurance of the afterlife and an example of Christ's teachings on earth. By the fourteenth century, the Church was woefully in deficit on its side of the social bargain.

This was an age of ostentatious clerical wealth. There were monks who were local drunks and priests who sought sexual

**For all its supposed piety, the Church of the late fourteenth
century was corrupt and decadent.**

favours. For a price, a couple could be illicitly wed, a blessing could
be bought and the 'holiest' of relics could change hands for the right
price. The Church of the thirteenth and fourteenth centuries was, in
its own terms, decadent and corrupt. This moral decay was reflected,
unsurprisingly, in a widespread scepticism in the authority of the
clergy and a corrosion of the respect that the Church needed in
order to survive. By the later fourteenth century Church revenues
were falling, churches closing and parishes being merged.

   In the thirteenth century, mendicant orders such as the
Franciscans had become enormously popular. The mendicants were
seen as oppositional to the Church by virtue of their chosen poverty
and the austerity of their lives. By the fourteenth century the
success of the mendicants, and the wealth they had attracted, had
corrupted them also. Stories abounded of the scandalous goings on
behind the cloistered walls of the monasteries and nunneries.

Resentment was rising at the constant fleecing of parish flocks and the pressure to support the friars and monks. It was said that folk dreaded the appearance of monks more than beggars because of the expectation of sustenance and contributions.

It seemed also that the clergy were more interested in their social advancement than in the salvation of souls, either their own or those of others. Increasingly, the clergy took up positions in the estates and homes of the wealthy. This process of secularization of the clergy is well observed in the literature of the time. The friar of Chaucer's *Canterbury Tales* is clearly a man of comfortable means. And Langland in *Piers Plowman* also makes clear his contempt for the hypocrisy of the friar:

> *For I have seyn hym in sylke, and somme tyme in russet,*
> *Bothe in grey and in grys* [grey squirrel-fur] *and in*
> *gulte herneys* [gilded armour]¹³

Langland's opinion of the corruption of the Church as well as the final fate of the clergy is equally clear:

Thus pey geuen here golde glotone to kepe,	So people hand over their money to maintain gluttons and put their
And leueth such loseles pat lecherye haunten.	faith in wastrels who practise lechery. If the bishop were a holy
Were pe biscop yblissed and worth bothe his eres,	man and worth his keep, his seal would not be sent out to deceive the
His seel shulde nouzt be sent to deceyue pe pepl . . .	people . . .
Some seruen pe kyng and his siluer tellen,	Some serve the king by reckoning up his money or by claiming, in the
In cheker and in chancerye chalengen his dettes	Exchequer or the Chancery, what is owing to him from wardships and
Of wardes and wardmotes, weyues and streyues.	ward-meetings, from property with no owner and from the estates left by
And some seruen as suruantz lordes and ladyes,	aliens. Some take service with lords and ladies and act as judges in the
And in stede of stuwardes sytten and emen.	manorial courts, in the place of stewards. Mass matins and many of

<table>
<tr><td>

Here messe and here matynes and
*   many of here oures*
Arn don vndeuoutlych; drede is at
*   pe laste*
Lest Crist in constorie acorse ful
manye . . .

</td><td>

their offices are said without
devotion. It is to be feared that, on
the Last Day, Christ, seated in His
consistory court, will place many of
them under His curse.[14]

</td></tr>
</table>

This degeneration of the Church and the consequent decay of its ideological hold on society was symptomatic of more fundamental changes that were occurring throughout the whole of society. Compared to the thirteenth century, society was becoming more complex. The ideological motif of the three groups in society – the workers, the fighters and the prayers – had given way to a new metaphor. People now spoke of society as a kind of mystical body. Thomas Brinton, the bishop of Rochester, described kings and princes as the head of society, judges as the eyes, clergy as the ears, doctors as the tongue, knights as the right hand, merchants and 'faithful artisans' as the left, burgesses and citizens as the heart, and the peasants, of course, as the feet 'supporting the entire body'.[15] There certainly was a greater social differentiation within feudal society by the fourteenth century. There were several distinct strata of traders, artisans and merchants. The peasants also were far more heterogeneous and there was even the phenomenon of the prosperous peasant family who were beginning to benefit from trade.

The slow cumulative changes and improvements in farming techniques and animal husbandry had by the thirteenth and fourteenth centuries created the conditions for a rapid growth of population. Population growth in turn stimulated productivity and had continued throughout the thirteenth century. In an age when human labour power was still a primary energy source, population growth was a driver of economic expansion. One result of this economic growth was a growth in trade. Many of the towns of modern-day England, with their town squares and triangles, began as the intersection of trading routes in the late medieval period. English merchants were trading way beyond English shores. From the ports of Bergen and Oslo came timber and fish, from Venice and Genoa came wines, silk, spices and glass, from Seville, Malaga and Lisbon came oil, iron, leather and wax, and from other parts of

Europe came rope, dyestuffs, cloth, salt, canvas, pitch and tar.[16] Probably the most advanced manufacturing centre in the medieval world at this time was Flanders, whose exports of fine muslins and luxury goods were unrivalled. England was known for the quality of its wool, and a well-developed trade between Flanders and England had emerged.

The growth of the towns and cities was an important development in English society. Although the populations of the towns were still small compared with that of the country as a whole, nonetheless they began to emerge as powerful economic and political centres. The burghers and merchants of the new market towns as well as some of the older cities that were outgrowing their Roman walls began to push increasingly for political independence. The status of 'free borough' allowed a town to shake off manorial and royal domination to some degree, to set its own taxes and to establish independent courts. As the burgher families grew in economic power and influence, so the tensions between the new urban centres and the older powers of the royal court and the Church also became more pronounced.[17]

Within the towns themselves, social tensions were also apparent. By the fourteenth century, powerful guilds had emerged. These guilds had grown up from the increasing trade specializations within the general urban expansion of the time. The most powerful and wealthy of the masters within the trade guilds were now rivalling the old families that had dominated town and city life for centuries. They began to push increasingly for inclusion within the political structures, and in many cities tensions between the established authorities and the guilds came to dominate public life. Within the guilds, originally set up to protect trade members in times of hardship and to regulate wages and competition, fragmentation was also evident. Guild members consisted of the masters – an increasingly privileged social layer – the apprentices and the journeymen. The journeymen were those who had finished their apprenticeships but had not yet become masters of their own workshops. By the fourteenth century, the numbers of journeymen who had no real hope of becoming masters had grown significantly. Such journeymen were effectively wage labourers and their interests were for the first time becoming openly antagonistic to

**By the time of the revolt, the traditional sense of reciprocity
between lord and peasant had broken down.**

those of the masters. In 1396 the saddlers' guild complained that its
journeymen were organizing separately with their own colours and
ceremonies in *covins* to raise their wages. In the late fourteenth
century much of the urban unrest and rioting that occurred was
associated with tensions within the guilds.

English society by the fourteenth century was one in which
immense forces of economic, social and ideological antagonism had
become locked together. The edifice of medieval society, with its
abbeys and manor houses, bore down too hard on the body of the
peasant. And to the eyes of the peasant, when they were able to look
up for a moment from their toil, that edifice no longer presented a
convincing picture, if it ever had. The wealth of the merchants as
well as the corruption of the Church gave rise to growing social
resentment and moral disgust. What the peasants saw gave the lie

more and more to what the priest preached to them from the pulpit. The contradictions of fourteenth-century society were setting the stage for revolution. These contradictions might have developed, with occasional outbursts of rebellion perhaps, but without revolution, for another century or two. The historical process was hastened, however, by the politics of the time and the actions of the ruling class – and by the forces of nature.

CHAPTER 2

THE MAKING OF THE REVOLT

The rise in population that had marked the later decades of the thirteenth century was, by the early fourteenth century, coming to an end. The rise had in part been self-stimulating. As the quantity of human labour power increased, so too did total production. This in turn provided the basis for further demographic growth. This could only occur up to a point, however, within the limitations of feudal productive techniques. By the turn of the century, population had started to decline as the output of food proved insufficient for the number of mouths to be fed. The early decades of the fourteenth century were marked by food shortage and famines as well as cattle plagues. In some parts of the kingdom of Edward I, social structures were breaking down as local gangs terrorized villages. A sense of crisis pervaded the already fragile world of medieval England. At the turn of the mid-century, however, a calamity of Old Testament proportions occurred which was to profoundly shape the history of the rest of the century.

The plague of 1348–9 struck on a scale and with a savagery that people could only explain as being an act of divine retribution by a vengeful God angry at the sinfulness of the human world. Its appearance from the East, from the lands of 'pilgrimage and crusade', gave it a demonic aspect in the mid-fourteenth century imagination. The expansion of trade between western Europe and the Orient had provided a new vehicle for the transmission of disease. The bacillus responsible for the plague was carried in the blood of the black rat and the vector for the transmission to humans was the common rat flea. These rats and their companions travelled on the boats of the growing grain trade.

By the end of 1347, the plague had arrived at Cyprus. The following month it had struck at Provence and Avignon. Already it had ravaged Italy and had reached far into Germany. In June of 1348 two ships from Gascony arrived in Melcombe Regis on the

Dorsetshire coast and the Black Death, as the Elizabethan historian John Stow was later to call it, made its first appearance in England.

The symptoms of the disease itself added to the terror. This was no sleeping sickness of slow fatigue and decline. Bubonic plague creates a disgusting effect on its victim. It strikes fast. Within two days the lymphatic areas of the neck, groin and armpits have swollen. These swellings, or buboes, begin to ooze vile-smelling pus. Black carbuncles also appear. One Welsh poet and victim described the effect:

> *It is seething, terrible, wherever it may come, a head that gives pain and causes a loud cry, a burden carried under the arms, a painful angry knob, a white lump. It is of the form of an apple, like the head of an onion, a small boil that spares no one. Great is its seething, like a burning cinder, a grievous thing of an ashy colour.*[1]

The victim died within a week, tortured by intense points of pain over their body. The plague is represented in the art of the fourteenth century by the figure of St Sebastian, who suffered death by arrows.

Once in England, the plague travelled swiftly. From Dorset it moved westwards and northwards. Bristol was the first major town to be ravaged. In vain, the Gloucestershire authorities attempted to prevent anybody entering from the direction of Bristol. Soon it had reached Oxfordshire. By 1 November 1348 the disease had worked its way back down the Thames into London. It appeared in Norwich in January of 1349. Over the next few months York, Lancashire and the northern districts of England and eventually Ireland were visited, before eventually the plague expired by the end of the summer.

Estimates vary considerably as to how many human souls were dispatched by the plague. A general consensus says that at least a third of the population of England died. Upper estimates put the figure at more like a half. The death toll also varied from one part of the country to the next. Certainly the church graveyards were quickly exhausted. The plague cemeteries that are marked today are only the sites of which we still have records. But one feature of the plague that should not surprise was that it affected the poor more

The panicked burial of victims of the plague did not stop it spreading at frightening speed throughout Europe.

than it affected the rich. Amongst the attendants of the House of Lords, for example, only 4½ per cent died in 1348 and 13 per cent the following year. Only one member of the royal household was struck down.[2] As in every age dominated by inequalities of wealth, the housing and lifestyles of the wealthy ensured that they remained relatively protected from the rats and fleas that brought death to the doors of the rest of the population.

The plague had immediate effects, both psychologically and socially, for those who survived. Some chronicles report a mentality of abandon and dissoluteness. More commonly though, the atmosphere in England seems to have been one of a strange malaise and an outlook of pessimism and deep despair.

> In these days was death without sorrow, wedding without friendship, wilful penance, and dearth without scarcity, and fleeing without refuge or succour.[3]

The longer-term consequences of the Black Death, however, were social and economic. Villages had been cleared and large areas of the country had become depopulated. With such a dearth of labour, harvests could not be brought in, despite women and children being put into the fields. Famine came in the shadow of disease. A dislocation now occurred in the economic relations that had prevailed on the manors. A loosening of the old loyalties and obligations began to develop. The villeins were now in a position to make demands. In particular, they insisted on payment for working the lord's land. The old habits of labour dues and customary working of the lord's *demesne* land were replaced more and more by waged labour.

Increasingly, villeins would 'flee' the manor on which they and their families before them had spent their whole lives, confident in the knowledge that they would find another lord or merchant landowner only too happy to hire them. In doing so they were breaking the customs, obligations and legal attachments to the land that had provided the basis of feudalism for generations. Many of the landowners would eventually choose forms of farming that relied less on human labour and far more on the grazing of animals. Sheep farming, in particular, was to become significant as peasants were driven off their lands for pasture and the market for mutton grew in the urban centres. More importantly, in our period, wool became a crucial export to Flanders and other centres of the early textile industry. It was also to become a dominating factor in the European political conflicts of the later fourteenth century.

The shortage of labour, caused by a plague that had affected the young and fit more than the old, began to make itself felt. It became possible now for a labourer to travel from one village and town to another and find work, particularly during the harvests. Trades people and artisans were especially in demand and the prices of manufactured goods rose accordingly. The price of food fell with fewer mouths to buy for. Chroniclers of the day commented on the phenomenon of the travelling labourer as almost a motif of the times. He represented a wanderlust that was significant on both a psychological and an ideological level as well as being important from an economic point of view. It was no longer only the travelling friars who moved around the country. Workmen also moved from place to place, carrying news of the places from whence they had come as well as occasional ideas and stories they had picked up along the way.

The plague had made labour a precious commodity for the first time on any serious scale and wages began to rise on the basis of the bargaining power of the labourer. After a century of growing differentiation and internal contradiction, the wealthiest classes now found unity in a common purpose – to stem the rising wage levels of the rural labourers and to break their rising confidence and social aspirations. The open struggle over wages and social status that had now begun was to define the English domestic social scene for the next thirty years.

The first act of the King in Council designed to push back wages to pre-plague levels was the Ordinance of 1349. It attempted to set wages at 1346 levels. This was given parliamentary backing in 1351 in the form of the Statute of Labourers. Under the statute, labourers were obliged to work for a lord for a whole year. Short time and day labouring, which in a time of labour shortage benefited the labourer, was declared unlawful. The argument used to recommend the statute was one that we can recognize today:

> . . . *because a great part of the people, and especially of workmen and servants, late died of the pestilence, many seeing the necessity of masters, and the great scarcity of servants, will not serve unless they may receive excessive wages, and some willing to beg in idleness* [rather] *than by labour to get a living; we considering the grievous incommodities, which of the lack especially of ploughmen and such labourers as may hereafter come, have upon deliberation and treaty of the prelates and the nobles and learned men assisting us . . . ordained . . . (1) Every ablebodied person under sixty 'not living in merchandise or exercising any craft, not having his own whereby he may live nor proper land' shall be bound to serve when required at no higher wage than in the 20th year of the reign* [of Edward III] . . . *or else be committed to prison . . .*[4]

The statute laid down the payment that could be given for every type of work: hay could be mown for 5d an acre; a quarter of wheat could be threshed for 2½d. Every craft – carpentry, metalwork, stone masonry, tailoring, etc. – was regulated in similar manner:

carters, ploughmen, leaders of the plough, shepherds, swineherds, domestic and all other servants shall receive the liveries and wages accustomed in the said twentieth year [of the reign of Edward III] *and four years previously; so that in areas where wheat used to be given, they shall take 10d for the bushel, or wheat at the will of the giver, unless it is ordained otherwise.*[5]

In every town 'ceppes' or stocks were to be placed for the punishment of those who attempted to raise their wages beyond these levels or who refused to take an oath of obedience to the statute.[6] Those who broke their oath would be imprisoned for forty days. Those who broke their oath for a second time would be imprisoned for a 'quarter of a year'. Thereafter the sentence would be doubled each time such a rebel was caught contravening the statute.

The Statute of Labourers was to be returned to again and again by Parliament over the next three decades to be elaborated and updated. In 1360 we see Parliament institute a new statute designed to control the mobility of labour and in particular to stamp out the phenomenon of the wandering labourer. Those labourers who were found to be straying too far from their ascribed place of residence were to have the letter 'F' for 'Falsity' branded on their foreheads. In 1361 local sheriffs were given greater and somewhat arbitrary powers to arrest all 'evil-doers, rioters and barrators'.[7]

Parliament was not only concerned with wages, however. As peasants gained in confidence with regard to their economic position, they also began to feel differently about the social hierarchy to which they were supposed to defer. Peasants now began to have aspirations 'above their station'. This was more than their betters could stomach and so was passed what must be regarded as one of the most openly and odiously class-conscious pieces of legislation in history. The Sumptuary Laws of 1363 attempted to lay down by parliamentary decree the standards of consumption for different classes in society. The types of clothing and diet to which each stratum within society had to restrict themselves were spelled out in detail. For example, those who worked at handicrafts and yeomen were not to wear *stone, cloth of silk or silver, girdle, knife, button, ring, garter, brooch, ribbon, chains or any manner of things of gold or silver, or any manner of apparel embroidered or enamelled, their wives and children similarly*

whereas

Carters, ploughmen, drivers of the plough, oxherds, cowherds, shepherds, dairyworkers, and all other keepers of beasts, threshers of corn . . . shall not take or wear any manner of cloth but blanket and russet wool of 12d, and shall wear girdles of linen according to their estate, and come to eat and drink as in the manner that pertain to them and not excessively.[8]

Such a statute could never be effectively implemented and the Sumptuary Laws were something of a dead letter from the outset. They were repealed two years later. In their very conception and enactment, however, they speak volumes about the conflict that was shaping social opinion in this period.

The attempts to hold down wages also proved to be ultimately unsuccessful. The Statute of Labourers could never really be effective and average wage rates continued to rise. The repeated attempts to enforce it, however, meant that it became not only a hated piece of class legislation but also the grist in a class struggle of a new type. Previously, peasants had struggled against a particular lord who oppressed them. Now their hostility was aimed increasingly at Parliament and other national institutions. The politicization that this made possible was to become generalized into a much more fundamental questioning of society.

By the 1370s the class antagonisms that had been unleashed by the Black Death were intensifying into a more generalized unrest. In the 1370s we see landlords and employers, unable to control the labour 'problem' on their estates unaided, petitioning Parliament for help. The appeals and statutes of the time give evidence of union and combination amongst the peasants as they both resisted the feudal reaction being waged by the late-fourteenth-century ruling class and pressed home their own demands. A statute of 1377 was passed in response to an appeal from 'the commons' regarding truculent labour on the estates:

These men have refused to allow the officials of the lords to distrain them for the said customs and services; and have made confederation and alliance together to resist the lords and officials by force, so that each will aid the other whenever they are distrained for any reason. And they threaten to kill their lord's servants if these make distraint upon them for their customs and services; the consequence is that, for fear of the deaths that might result from the rebellion and resistance of these men, the lords and their officials do not make distraint for their customs and services. Accordingly the said lords lose and have lost much profit from their lordships, to the great prejudice and destruction of their inheritances and estates.[9]

Amongst the well-to-do a fearfulness of the peasantry and a growing anxiety about the threat they represented is apparent. Their imaginations were still dimly haunted by the *Jacquerie* – the bloody uprisings of the French peasantry in 1358. By the late 1370s there was certainly a sense of impending catastrophe. But economics alone cannot explain the storm that was soon to break. The consciousness that was emerging amongst the 'lower orders' was focused by a growing antagonism towards not only the 'higher orders' but actually the very 'highest' in the land. The sharpness of the class conflict that was brewing was quickened by the politics of the time.

By the mid-1370s the reign of Edward III was disintegrating. Edward himself was in his dotage and already senile. He had retreated into a private inner court with his mistress, the universally unpopular Alice Perrers, who had arrogated her own social and political influence as the king's favourite. The real power behind the throne was a man who dominated the political life of England – John of Gaunt.

John of Gaunt was easily the most powerful individual in England in the period immediately before the outbreak of the Peasants' Revolt. He was by far the largest landowner with lordships stretching from Liddel and Dunstanburgh on the Scottish border to Kingston Lacey and Willingdon on the south coast of England, and from Gimmingham and Aylsham on the East Anglian coast to Monmouth and Kidwelly in Wales.[10] He was third son to the king and the brother of the ageing heir to the throne, Edward of Wales –

the Black Prince. John of Gaunt raised his own private armies when
he set out on one of his many military expeditions to Scotland,
France or Spain.

> *He was probably the mightiest subject England has ever seen.*
> *The Duchy of Lancaster was an independent palatinate within*
> *whose boundaries the King's writ did not run. In addition*
> *Gaunt possessed countless rich estates and properties*
> *throughout England, ranging from a vast sheep ranch in the*
> *Peak District to his splendid palace of the Savoy just outside the*
> *City. His revenues and his retinue were scarcely surpassed by*
> *those of his father. Moreover, as the husband of Pedro the*
> *Cruel's daughter he was rightful King of Castile.*[11]

John of Gaunt, however, also faced a challenge to his power in the
form of an institution that was beginning to play a more
independent and critical role. As society had become more complex
and heterogeneous in terms of its class composition, Parliament
began to change too in terms of the interests that it represented.
Previously, parliaments had consisted of gatherings of lords and
senior gentry summoned by the king and his council and elected
gentry from the counties and shires whose purpose, in broad terms,
was to approve the king's law and to set taxes. The 'Good
Parliament', however, which began in April 1376 and lasted until
July 1376, was not only the longest running parliament that had
assembled. It was also a focal point for tensions that were reaching
breaking point within the political establishment. The towns and
shires had sent up representatives who were critical of what they
regarded as the abuse of royal powers. An antagonism quickly
opened up between the members of the Good Parliament and John
of Gaunt.

The Good Parliament complained about the corruption
surrounding the king and his clique. The most powerful magnates in
London had been able, through court influence and manipulation of
the enfeebled monarch, to secure highly lucrative monopolies and
financial arrangements for themselves. London financiers such as
Richard Lyons, Adam Bury, John Peeche and John Pyel were all
charged with having sold licences to merchants for the avoidance of
tax on goods passing through the Calais 'staple' and with having

arranged loans to the crown at exorbitant rates of interest. The fact that this parliament was able to score victories, albeit temporary, over John of Gaunt and the royal court betrayed rumblings occurring deeper within society. This parliament was reflecting the interests of a new and ever-growing mix of smaller merchants and lower gentry who wished to check the power of the court over their social and business affairs. When Peter de la Mare, speaker for the Good Parliament, laid out the chief grievances to John of Gaunt and said that the 'king has with him certain councillors and servants who are not loyal or profitable to him or the kingdom',[12] he considered himself to be speaking for the 'Commons of England' and not for one particular group. The Good Parliament was eventually closed by John of Gaunt. The crisis surrounding Gaunt, however, did not subside. But now his conflict was with the Church.

The Church of late-fourteenth-century Europe was undergoing its own political crisis. Since 1309 the papacy had been caught within the 'Babylonish captivity'. This referred to the fact that France, the largest and most politically powerful region in Europe, had brought the papacy from Rome to Avignon. This gave the French monarchy an immensely important lever of political influence inside every other country. It gave the French ruling class, for instance, the power to appoint bishops and prelates of its own choosing into key positions in England. A proportion of the taxes raised in England were also sent to Avignon to support the Church. The tensions that were opening up between different European countries with the growth of trade were now becoming focused, within England, on an increasing opposition to the Church.

The reoccupation of Rome by the Italians paved the way for the return of the papacy to its historic home by 1370. It was the papacy of Urban VI, however, and the anti-French reforms that became associated with it, which was to split the Church for nearly half a century. In 1378 a group of cardinals returned to Avignon and appointed their own pope, Clement VII.[13] The great 'schism' meant that two popes now ruled God's kingdom on Earth. Now the different emerging powers on the western European continent lined up around these two poles. The Spanish, the English and the Italians supported the Pope in Rome. The Scots and the Neapolitans supported the Pope at Avignon. The Church had never been above politics. But now this was obvious to the most uneducated peasant in the furthest flung reaches of the Church's influence. The mystical power of the key ideological institution in medieval society, which had dominated the mind of Europe for centuries, was shattered.

The crisis of the Church was not only political. The voices that questioned the authority of the Church were becoming more numerous, louder and more confident in the late fourteenth century. Numerous cults surrounding saints, visionaries and holy figures had emerged. In Europe the manias surrounding Brigitta of Sweden and Catherine of Siena had posed fundamentalist challenges to Church authorities. The Apostles, in particular, became objects of adoration and popular affection as figures who were 'more like us' than the bishops and cardinals. In England the cult of Thomas à Becket and the popular trade in relics betrayed an erosion of religious awe for the established Church. The crisis of Christian ideology, however, was occurring on a much more profound level and right in the heart of the intellectual establishment. One name above all others stands out as being of key importance in this part of the story – that of John Wycliffe.

John Wycliffe was a senior figure at Oxford University who, for a time, had been Master of Balliol College. He was one of a line of Oxford schoolmen who had been dissenters from Church orthodoxy on theological matters. Ockham before him had put forward views that favoured the restriction of theological authority to religious and spiritual matters. But Wycliffe's teachings, resonating through the immense contradictions of the fourteenth century, rang louder in the ears of his contemporaries – and in every part of society. He preached against the wealth and ostentation of the official Church. He castigated the abbots and friars for their corruption and he appealed to a fundamentalist sentiment that was at large in society and which made him a popular figure.

It was Wycliffe's theological teachings, however, which attracted the attention of the authorities in Rome. He denied the transubstantiation of the Eucharist, which struck directly against the power that the priest and friar held over their congregates. He denied the Pope's authority over men's souls. In his doctrine of 'Dominion' he declared that God dispensed grace to men according to the state of their souls and not according to a pre-ordained station in life. Mortal sin broke this state of grace and therefore the right of

The universities were hotbeds of intellectual debate and dissent.

all temporal authority. He advocated the abolition of the Pope and Church authorities. He inspired and was partly responsible for the writing of the first English translation of the Bible. In 1377 a Papal Bull was issued against Wycliffe which asserted that:

> *The heretic was standing for England against Rome, for the State against the Church . . . that he had declared against the power of the Pope to bind and loose* [the souls of men], *and had maintained that excommunication when unjust had no real effect. He had pronounced it the duty of the State to secularise the property of the Church when she grew too rich, in order to purify her. He said that any ordained priest had the power to administer any of the Sacraments, several of which the Roman Catholic Church reserves to Bishops alone.*[14]

Wycliffe's influence was of European significance. He directly influenced Jan Huss and the peasant communist movements on the continent. But in England, Wycliffe became inevitably embroiled in the contemporary political struggle. John of Gaunt saw in Wycliffe a powerful weapon against the Church in England and so took him under his protection. When Wycliffe was summoned by the bishops at St Paul's Cathedral to answer the charges of the Papal Bull, crowds gathered to support him. When John of Gaunt appeared, however, as Wycliffe's protector, the mood changed completely. Rioting occurred and Gaunt was forced to flee for his life. The first bubbles were appearing in the pot that was soon to boil over.

The overlapping crises both within and between the politics of state and those of religion reverberated downwards to meet the rising discontent emerging from the base of society. What hastened this situation was the issue of taxation. For most of the fourteenth century England had been at war. This was the period of what historians were to call the 'Hundred Years War', which lasted in its different phases from 1337 to 1453. The year 1369 had seen the end of a nine-year peace and the war since then had not gone well for the English armies in France. The French expeditions had to be paid for and by 1375 the resumption of war had cost the treasury £650,000.[15] In practically its last act during the reign of Edward III, the parliament of 1377, a parliament now loyal to John of Gaunt, declared a tax of 4d on every person over fourteen years of age.

Traditionally the villeins had been spared direct taxation by the state and the injustice of the new tax was not lost on the poorest in society. This poll tax was to be followed by two others.

The scene was set for revolution when Richard of Bordeaux came to the throne in 1377 at the age of ten. But this historical moment might still have passed were it not for one final essential ingredient – the patient work of revolutionaries. Throughout England there were poor priests who were close to their parishioners and who shared the sense of outrage and social injustice of their times. Such priests were frequently influenced by Wycliffite ideas. Certainly they were impressed by Wycliffe's support for the collective non-payment of taxes that were considered to be unfair, and many were the priests who actively led their flocks in such resistance. There were friars also who preached a levelling doctrine. The most popular expression of this appeal for a human equality on Earth to match that in heaven drew on a radical image of the Garden of Eden. Often a sermon by a local or travelling priest would include the couplet:

> *When Adam delved and Eve span,*
> *Who was then a gentleman?*

God had not created classes. This was the work of humankind. And what had not been made by God could be unmade by human beings. Versions of this rhyme can be found all over Europe at different times in this historical epoch. There were some, however, who had been preaching such sentiments well before the late 1370s and well before the influence of Wycliffe and his itinerant priests. The most important of these was John Ball, who had begun his career twenty years previously. He was known to the authorities, who repeatedly tried to silence him. Ball was no stranger to the inside of a fourteenth-century prison. But nothing would deter him. He attacked Church and State alike with a militant rhetoric and was awarded the predictable title of the 'Mad Priest of Kent' by his enemies. He attacked in particular the indignities of bondage and serfdom. We have a record of his style of speech and the notions that inspired him and his listeners:

> *He was accustomed every Sunday after Mass, as the people were*

John Ball was the spiritual leader of the rebellion. He preached that in the Garden of Eden there had been no such thing as 'rich and poor'.

coming out of church, to preach to them in the market-place and assemble a crowd around him, to whom he would say, 'My good friends, things cannot go well in England, nor ever will until everything shall be in common; when there shall be neither vassal nor lord and all distinctions levelled, when lords shall be no more masters than ourselves. How ill have they used us? And for what reason do they hold us in bondage? Are we not all descended from the same parents, Adam and Eve? And what can they show or what reasons give, why they should be more masters than ourselves? except perhaps in making us labour and work for them to spend. They are clothed in velvets and rich stuffs, ornamented with ermine and other furs, while we are forced to wear poor cloth. They have handsome seats and manors, when we must brave the wind and rain in our labours in the field; but it is from our labour that they have wherewith to support their pomp. We are called slaves, and if we do not perform our services we are beaten.[16]

It was such ideas that raised the imagination of the villeins beyond their most immediate concerns and fused their social anger with a new and utopian vision. That vision was creating a revolutionary consciousness and the revolution that this had made possible was about to begin.

CHAPTER 3

THE REVOLT BEGINS

By 1380 the costs of the wars in France were crippling the English state and the wars themselves had gone badly for Richard's armies. No thought of ending the campaigns troubled the minds of the good lords who assembled in Parliament that winter, however. Meeting in Northampton, for fear of the hostility of the London population, they discussed instead the ways by which they might raise more revenues for the further prosecution of the war. Two poll taxes, those of 1377 and 1379, had already been levied on the population and had provoked widespread resentment. A third tax was now proposed and, after some alternatives had been considered and dismissed, was agreed.

The tax was set at 3 groats – 1 shilling – for every person of the realm above the age of fifteen. This was far in excess of the previous two poll taxes. In 1377 a tax of 1 groat had been levied and in 1379 the tax had been graduated according to income. The new tax was also to be graduated according to the wealth of the area. But in 1381 the wealthy of most regions were not of a mind to be generous and were determined that the vast bulk of the revenue should come from the villeins. This meant that even the very poorest peasants would have to pay the same 3 groats as the richest landowners.

The first resistance to the poll tax of 1381 was massive evasion. The wastefulness of the war and the unfairness of the tax was producing a growing resentment amongst the villeins. As returns came in, the poll tax commissionaires began to notice a remarkable fact. The population of England, it seemed, had fallen considerably! In Kent, for example, the roll of 1377 had shown a population of 56,557 whereas it now appeared to have fallen to 43,838. In Somerset it had fallen even more, from 54,604 in 1377 to 30,384. In Devon more than half the 1377 population had disappeared, the roll falling from 45,635 to 20,656. Across the whole country the population seemed to have fallen from 1,355,201 in 1377 to

896,481 in 1381.[1] This scale of evasion and the fact that it occurred over most of the country suggests more than a merely spontaneous response to this oppressive third tax. It seems likely that a level of organization and coordination was involved. This was something that the rich and well-to-do could barely conceive of – that these villeins, these barely human creatures, might be capable of such initiative and planning. And yet the returns suggested just that.

In fact, planning had been afoot for some time. The Magna Societas, or Great Society, had been plotting rebellion well before the revolt itself. Infused with a radical Christian levelling doctrine, its centre was almost certainly Colchester, the home town of John Ball. In some parts it was likely to have been organized with local leaderships and communication between towns. In other parts it was probably no more than an idea, an understanding that a great change was soon to come. But by the spring of 1381 it was no longer just a dream. The Great Society, the mass of feudal England, was on the move.

By March the king had been forced to dismiss the tax commissionaires amidst accusations of corruption and collusion with the peasants. A new body of collectors was appointed with much greater powers of arrest and punishment, and the deadline for the return of the full amount of £66,666 was brought forward from 2 June to 21 April. By the end of May around 83 per cent of this had been collected.[2]

England was by now seething with unrest. Mass desertions had occurred from many villages, and groups of peasants began to merge and travel from town to town in great convoys. And as they moved along the country roads, they discussed their situation. Stories were swapped about the aggressive impositions of the tax collectors and the injustices that had been visited upon their villages. Some told of the lecherous manner in which some tax collectors had inquired after the ages of young women and carried out their 'puberty test' by checking the growth of pubic hair. Others told of how their neighbours had been imprisoned for refusing to pay the tax twice.

As they contemplated the state of England and their general condition, the peasants' sense of resentment and hatred of those who had done these things became more and more intense. We can imagine how they might have sung the popular songs of their day, full of social anger and protest. Poems such as 'The Outlaw's Song of Trailbaston' described the injustice of false accusation and imprisonment by unscrupulous lords. 'Song of the Husbandman' spoke of the oppression of taxes in times of hardship for the peasants. The ballad of 'Adam Bell, Clim of the Clough and William of Cloudesley' celebrated the heroism of ordinary men who refuse to be put down by the rich and powerful. Some storytellers might have recounted the tales of Robin Hood.[3]

With every step they took and with every injustice remembered, these peasants gained in their sense of the righteousness of their actions. What also grew was their confidence. As each group of villages discovered that they were not alone, and as their realization of their strength also increased, they dared to imagine a final settling of things with those they now clearly saw as their social enemies. These peasants had gone beyond the point of no return. Already they were beyond the law. More and more they listened to the arguments of the radical voices amongst them and increasingly they began to share a vision of what might be.

In May 1381 electrical storms occurred across most of England and the thunder clouds and heavy air carried portent of what was to come. As the peasants marched and met by torchlight, they troubled the sleep of the rich. Amongst the ruling class a deep foreboding and depression descended. It was whispered that things were not well in the land and there were those who recalled the massacres of the nobles of France in 1358. Statutes passed in the period immediately before the revolt reflect these fears. One complained of

> *Devisors of false news and reports of horrible and false lies concerning prelates, dukes, earls, barons, and other noble and great men of the realme, and also concerning the Chancellor, Treasurer, Clerk of the Privy Seal, Steward of the Kings House, Justice of the one Bench or the other and of other great offices of the realme about things, which by the said nobles, prelates, lords and officers aforesaid were never spoken done nor thought . . . whereby debates and discords might arise betwixt the said lords and Commons which God forbid, and whereby great mischief might come to all the realme and quick subversion and destruction of the said realme, if due remedy be not provided . . .[4]*

By late May the die was cast. The visionaries of the Great Society were no longer preaching to small groups on village greens. They were now talking, directly and indirectly, to the multitude of the poorest parts of the population. Even the middle layers of society were being won over as this movement-in-waiting swelled. It was against this background that the tax commissionaire Thomas Bampton rode into Brentwood. Arriving with all the indifferent aloofness of his class, he summoned the people of the surrounding villages of Fobbing, Corringham and Stanford-le-Hope before him to account for their low returns. They arrived at his commission on 31 May, but not as he had expected. These fishing folk stood before him armed. When Thomas Baker of Fobbing spoke angrily to the London tax collector, denouncing the tax and refusing to pay, Bampton ordered his arrest. Immediately he and his entourage of clerks and soldiers were attacked and all were showered with stones as they fled from the town. The rising had begun.

With a speed that again suggests prior planning, word was sent to London and two emissaries of the Great Society, Adam Atwell and Roger Harry, soon after arrived to organize the revolt. All of the surrounding towns and villages were called upon to rise and by 1 June the rebels were meeting in the forests of Essex to arm themselves and discuss their strategy. The following day Sir Robert Belknap arrived with troops to impose order. Oblivious to the real scale of what was afoot and assuming this to be one more local nuisance to be solved with the usual judicious dose of floggings and perhaps a hanging, he was unprepared for what came next.

By messenger and hilltop fire, intelligence had been sent to the men of Kent that the Great Society was in motion. The military experience of the French wars, which until this time had only been good for public house boasting, was now put to different use. Swords came down from the wall, axes were sharpened, armour was cleaned and polished, and bows were re-strung. When Belknap arrived in Brentwood he was met by 500 peasants of Essex and Kent ready for battle. Belknap himself was tied to his horse backwards and ridden out of the town. The two ill-advised gentlemen who had volunteered as jurors to speak against the peasants were beheaded, their heads being tied to a horse and, in a manner of speaking, also run out of town.

Legend has it that the movement in Kent was started by a certain John Tyler of Dartford – not the Wat Tyler who is soon too play so prominent a part in our story. John Tyler, we are told, was at work when word came to him that his family and young daughter had been harassed by a tax collector, and so,

> *being at work in the same town tyling of an house, when he heard therof* [of the tax-collecting], *caught his lathing staff in his hand and ran reaking* [riotously] *home; where, reasoning with the collector who made him so bold, the collector answered with stout words and strake at the tyler; whereupon the tyler avoiding the blow, smote the collector with the lathing staff that the brains flew out of his head. Whereupon great noise arose in the street, and the poor people, being glad, everyone prepared to support the said John Tyler.*[5]

All over Essex and Kent, villages and towns were now assembling under quickly established leaders. At Erith, Abel Ker led his followers into the monastery at Lesness and forced the abbot to swear the first recorded oath to the 'True Commons'. At Canterbury, John Legge, the devisor of the poll tax, arrived with the king's commission to levy the tax. Battle briefly ensued at the West Gate of the city and Legge was driven out. At each village they visited, the peasants searched and destroyed the manorial rolls. These were the legal documents that recorded the status of the local peasants – whether they were free or unfree, their tithes to the lord and their tribute to the abbey and so on. This was no blind rebellion. The peasants had a purpose and that purpose was to destroy serfdom – the very basis of the feudal order. Indeed, the rolls also recorded the obligations of the lord, what few there were, and it is an indication of just how far the peasants had come that they were no longer concerned with the protection of their 'rights' within the prison of feudalism. The flames that consumed the parchment rolls would also, they hoped, destroy the chains of bondage.

On 5 June the peasants of Essex and Kent were at Dartford, where more peasants of the locality joined the growing army. Now under the leadership of the baker Robert Cave, they set off to Rochester, where the population was already in a state of excitement. The cause of the commotion at Rochester was the incarceration of one Robert Belling of nearby Gravesend. Sir Simon de Burley, a man notorious for his contempt towards the lower orders, claimed that Belling was a serf of his estate who had run away from bondage. The knight had had the man arrested and taken to the castle. It was a scene that must have been enacted over and over again in previous years. But now a different mood was abroad. The peasants of Gravesend were not of a mind to let such injustice prevail. As they combined with the Essex and Kent rebels, they became determined to free Belling and take the castle.

It is worth pausing for a moment on the significance of this early episode in the rebellion. Rochester Castle was no ordinary fortress. It had been the site of fortifications since Roman times and had always guarded the Medway bridge and the chief road for continental trade with London. The castle itself was one of the early achievements of the Norman military engineers, standing taller than any other castle in the land and with walls in places 4 metres thick. It was the boast of the English ruling class. It had never fallen to a foreign enemy and any French or other army seeking to invade England and reach London from the south would have to contend with its defences. To the local people Rochester Castle was a symbol of the power of the feudal system over their lives. It dominated the landscape and its dungeons were filled with those who had stolen from hunger or who had escaped bondage or who had simply and inadvertently fallen foul of the law. It now became the focus of a generation of social grievance against the feudal order.

Robert Cave and his men laid siege to Rochester Castle on the morning of 6 June. After several hours and a number of attempts upon the castle by the rebels, the constable, Sir John Newton, gave up the battle as lost and the peasant army charged through the gate to release Belling and the other prisoners.

> They laid strong siege to the castle, and the constable defended himself vigorously for half a day, but at length for fear that he had of such tumult, and because of the mad multitude of folks from Essex and Kent, he yielded to them.[6]

John Newton himself was later to be used as a messenger to the king. The psychological impact of these events cannot be overstated

— both upon the ruling class as well as upon the peasants themselves. Only a few days before, the lords of England had regarded the peasants as little more than labouring beasts of the land. They had been outraged at the effrontery of the peasants when they had chafed at the economic and social restrictions put upon them and had demanded more from their lot. And now these very same peasants, not content with defying the king's tax and causing disturbance and riot within the realm, had stormed and taken one of the key fortresses of England. The shock this produced went to the gut of the English ruling class.

The peasants also were suddenly struck by the magnitude of their actions. Whether things had been planned to go in this fashion or whether the taking of the castle was an unexpected turn of events we will never know. But certainly from this point on the rising became a profoundly serious affair. The fall of Rochester Castle became a clarion call to the peasants throughout England to rise and it is from this moment that the rebellion became a threat to the ruling class, not just on a local but also on a national scale.

As the rising spread, all forces were now making their way towards Maidstone. They were heading there to free John Ball, the spiritual leader of the rebellion. He had been imprisoned in Maidstone jail in April by Simon Sudbury, who was both Archbishop of Canterbury and also the chancellor. When he had been sentenced, Ball had announced that he would soon be freed by 20,000 men.

Maidstone was already in the hands of local rebels when the armies of Kent and the surrounding districts converged there on 7 June. As the peasants had passed through the towns and villages of southern England, they had ransacked the manor houses they had come across and had systematically destroyed all legal documents and manor rolls pertaining to lord–tenant relations. The peasants had shown remarkable restraint in their dealings with the lords and their families, and deaths were few and far between. The most violent of the events of the rising were soon to occur in London against key individuals who had already been identified as enemies of the people. This was no blind bloodlust. This was a movement with a very clear aim – to end the social basis of serfdom.

Maidstone now became the site of a conference at which the rebels discussed their aims. The peasants' loyalty was not to the rotten clique who surrounded the 14-year-old king, but rather to

'King Richard and the Commons of England'. John of Gaunt was named as a chief enemy of the people – they would accept 'no king named John'. War was declared upon power and privilege. They would rid the king of his corrupt councillors and would put to death all who upheld the law of Gaunt. All manorial and court rolls were to be destroyed. Those responsible for administering the injustice of the Statute of Labourers and general feudal law would meet stern retribution at the hands of the revolutionaries.

It was at the Maidstone conference also that Wat Tyler stepped out of obscurity on to the pages of history. It is sometimes wrongly stated that the individual plays no decisive role in history, compared to the great underlying forces of the historical process. The example of Wat Tyler gives the lie to this, if any example were needed. His historical role was to last only nine days, from the time of his election as leader of the rebellion at Maidstone on 7 June to his murder on 15 June at Smithfield. But in those nine days he changed the course of English history.

We know astonishingly little about the Wat Tyler himself. It is thought that he had been a soldier in the French wars. Certainly he had military skill, as our story will show. It is probable that he was a workman of some kind. He may have been a tiler as his name suggests, although by the late fourteenth century a surname was not a reliable guide to a person's occupation. We have no likeness of him. We know from chronicles that he was a gifted orator and had a quick tongue. There is also a story that as a younger man he had been a page to Richard Lyons, who was later executed by the rebels. It is likely, however, that this was a tale put about to trivialize Tyler's motives. Whatever the truth, we can be sure of one thing. His followers trusted him completely and were right to do so. He was of them and for them. He had their passionate fury at the injustice of lordly oppression, but was also able to express it and harness it with brilliant tactical skill.

With the election of Wat Tyler the movement began to organize on a higher level. John Ball was by now sending out letters to counties all over England. These letters are interesting in themselves. They were instructions to rise, certainly. But they were more than that. They told the people how to rise. These bulletins conveyed the urgency of the situation without ambivalence. The style of the letters was allegorical and couched in religious sentiments, but the message is clear: 'Now is the time', 'do not delay', 'organise yourselves' . . .

> *John Ball greeteth you all,*
> *And doth to understand he hath rung your bell,*
> *Now with might and right, will and skill,*
> *God speed every dell.*

He warns the peasants of each region to beware of betrayal, to stand together and to appoint only one leader to ensure the best possible discipline and organization:

> *John Shepe,*[7] *sometime St Mary priest of York, and now in Colchester, greeteth well John Nameless and John Miller and John Carter, and biddeth them that they beware of guile in borough and standeth together in God's name and biddeth Piers Plowman to go to his work and chastise well Hob the Robber,*[8] *and take with him John Trueman and all his fellows* [trustworthy men] *and no more, and look that ye shape to one head and no more.*

Things are not right in England, he says. Corruption is everywhere. Money and acquisition are put before the needs of the people. The Church is full of self-seeking and hypocrisy:

> *Now reigneth price in price,*
> *Covetise is holden wise,*
> *Lechery without shame,*
> *Gluttony without blame,*
> *Envy reigneth with reason*
> *And sloth is taken in great season.*
> *God do bote* [exact the penalty] *for now is time.*

The preparations have been made in fine detail, Ball explains to his reader. God is on our side and with steadfastness of purpose and the strength of our numbers we cannot fail. But they must keep a clear head and look out for traitors. They should choose only those they know to be loyal to the rising and no more. They should not look out only for themselves, but should remain pure of purpose and 'do well' and 'do better':

> *John Miller asketh help to turn his mill right:*
> *He hath ground small, small,*
> *The King's Son of Heaven will pay for it all,*
> *Look the mill go right, with its four sails dight.*
> *With right and with might, with skill and with will,*
> *And let the post stand in steadfastness,*
> *Let right help might, and skill go before will,*
> *Then shall our mill go aright.*
> *But if might go before right, and will go before skill*
> *Then is our mill mis-a-dight.*
> *Beware ere ye be woe.*
> *Know your friend from your foe*
> *Take enough and cry Ho!*
> *And do well and better and flee from sin,*[9]
> *And seek out peace and dwell therin,*
> *So biddeth John Trueman and all his friends.*

And everyone must be clear, he insists, that there is no turning back:

> *Jack Carter prays you all that ye make good end of what ye have*
> *begun and doeth well and aye better and better.*[10]

These letters and others like them were copied and distributed to all of the localities. They were carried in the pockets of peasants as they moved with increasing purpose towards the centres of power in fourteenth-century England, and must have been frequently taken out and read aloud to eager ears. Many were the peasants who went to the gallows after the suppression of the rising, carrying one of Ball's letters on their person.

The rebels now went about their business with a new clarity about the tasks they had set for themselves. A group of the rebels under Tyler's command set out to Canterbury where they hoped to find the Archbishop, Simon Sudbury, and settle accounts with him. As they travelled, they encountered pilgrims returning from the city, often having been to pay homage to the shrine of Thomas à

Becket. These pilgrims welcomed the message of the rebels, swore their oath to the commons and carried on their way, but now as emissaries of the peasants' cause.

Wat Tyler arrived in Canterbury on 10 June. The city rose up to welcome him and to declare themselves for the commons. After having feasted as guests of the city, the rebels headed for Sudbury's palace. The palace was ransacked and all of the palace documents and records were burned on a giant bonfire. Disappointed in not finding Sudbury himself, they next made for Canterbury Cathedral. The monks of the cathedral were terrified by the sight of Tyler and his men as they marched beneath the giant arches of the cathedral right up the aisle to where they were saying mass. The monks were spared, but the rebels announced that they should prepare for the coronation of a new archbishop very soon. Sudbury, they said, was to be executed, and John Ball, the priest of the common people, put in his place. Tyler now set out to rejoin the main peasant army still at Maidstone, but not before swearing the mayor and bailiffs of the city to uphold the principles of the Great Society. The town council took heed and began to organize things according to the new philosophy.

By this stage, all over Kent, the peasants had stamped their authority on the land. During the long summer days of 8, 9 and 10 June, manorial rolls had been destroyed in their thousands, prisoners had been released and the great houses of the lords had been set ablaze. The peasants were now ready to take their message to the king himself and to seek out those whom they regarded as the traitors of England. The peasants returned to Rochester and thence began their march to London.

The march to London was to take two days. These were two days during which the peasants again had the chance to contemplate what they had begun. With Canterbury, Dartford, Maidstone, Rochester and the other Kentish towns in peasant hands, they were now going to the capital to settle accounts with their enemies. Their minds were set on political ends. Again we have to stress that this was no irrational outburst of undirected anger. The peasants' consciousness of what they were doing and what they wanted to achieve was at a high level. The leaders had been able to communicate to their followers what was afoot and even the slowest of the peasants basically understood that their aims were social and political, and that attempts to use the movement for looting and personal gain would be dealt with sternly in this revolutionary army. The peasants were very clear about whom their quarrel was with.

In a slightly bizarre twist to our story, it seems that the king's mother may have even owed her life to the sense of higher purpose with which the peasants marched. On their journey to Canterbury to do worship at the tomb of her dead husband, the Black Prince, she and her entourage crossed the path of the peasant army at Eltham. They were convinced that they would perish at the hands of the peasants and gave themselves up for lost. Instead, after some rough jest and ribaldry, to their amazement they were allowed to go on their way.

On the night of 12 June, Wat Tyler's army arrived at Blackheath, south of the Thames. At least 30,000 peasants made camp for the night there. On the other side of the river the Essex army, which was at least as large as the Kentish army, was encamped at Mile End under the leadership of Jack Straw. They knew that tomorrow they would enter London. Faces lit by their fires, the peasants talked into the night. The London population, itself no more than 50,000, they knew, supported them. They talked of those to whom they would dispense justice and reminded each other of the reasons. Perhaps they joked about whether the other army had done as well. Perhaps they quarrelled about how things would go the next day. Perhaps also, with a mixture of excitement and apprehension, they wondered about the new society that was to come.

CHAPTER 4

THE TAKING OF LONDON

As the peasants camped outside London, the king and his advisers held desperate conference in the Tower of London, where they had moved for the security it offered on 11 June. Present with the king were Simon Sudbury and Robert Hales, who were both high on the list of figures with whom the peasants wished to deal. Also present were the earls of Arundel, Oxford, Warwick and Salisbury and the young Henry Bolingbroke, son of John of Gaunt.[1] This group must have presented a pathetic sight on the night of 12 June. They did not know how to act. The pace and scale of events had utterly overwhelmed them and they had taken no effective measures, so far, to quell the rising. Politically they were isolated. They had considered raising an army from the London population, but the reality was that in the present situation the loyalty of such a force could not be guaranteed. Finally, effectively admitting the impotence of their position, they decided to send word to the peasants to enquire what their grievances might be.

The rebels' reply was carried to the king by the knight John Newton, whom the rebels had taken prisoner after the capture of Rochester Castle. It rang with a confidence and clarity that stood in stark contrast to their own feeble communication. The peasants had risen 'to save the king and to destroy the traitors to him and the kingdom'.[2] A second communication came from behind the walls of the Tower. Might the peasants perhaps wait a day before carrying out their stated task, whilst the king spoke directly to the leaders of the rising? This was agreed and a meeting was planned for the next day, 13 June, at a place near Rotherhithe. In fear of the king's personal safety, Richard was to be taken on a barge down the Thames to meet the rebels and perhaps to reason with them and so avert catastrophe.

We should pause to consider this extraordinary moment. We have already seen the attitude that the lords and nobles had towards

Aware of the danger they were in, the king and his nobles desperately debated the few options available to them.

their villeins. Yet here was the king of England bowing to the peasants by allowing himself to be taken not only to meet with them, but actually to negotiate with them about their grievances. The scene seems astonishing to us. It must have been even more astonishing to the noble lords that Wednesday evening.

13 June was the feast of Corpus Christi and the peasants at Blackheath rose early to hear mass from John Ball. We can only guess at the thoughts that must have been in Ball's mind as he surveyed his congregation that summer morning. Tens of thousands of faces were turned towards him, faces filled with excitement and with a wondering about what would happen now. The importance of this auspicious day must have struck him powerfully. But if he was

On the morning of 13 June, Ball addressed the rebel armies before they took London.

an emotional man, he did not let this affect him. A great and dangerous undertaking was under way and it was his responsibility to convey to the rebels how the day would go and how the rising should be conducted.

Ball's sermon was more than merely a blessing before battle. With all of the peasant rebels from Kent and also from Surrey, Sussex, Hampshire and other counties of south-east England present, many of whom had only become involved in the rising in the last day or two, this was the moment to raise their sights to the highest level and to weld this army together in single purpose. He began with his familiar theme of Adam and Eve. Lords and serfs had not been created by God. In the happy state represented by the Garden of Eden, Adam delved and Eve span. According to the Bible, in the beginning there were only workers. Classes had been created by man and were a distortion of God's design.

This Christian communism tapped a deep sentiment amongst the commoners. But now was the time to make this idea more than just a sentiment. The rebels wished to see it become a reality.

There was work to be done and after warning of the tricks and deceits their enemies might attempt, Ball began to bring the philosophical idealism of the revolt together with their practical objectives:

> *by the word of that proverb which he took for his theme, to introduce and prove, that from the beginning all men were made alike by nature, and that bondage and servitude was brought in by oppression of naughty men against the will of God. For if it had pleased God to have made bondsmen he would have appointed them from the beginning of the world, who should be slave and who lord. They sought to consider, therefore, that now was a time given to them by God, in the which, laying aside the continual bondage, they might if they would, enjoy their long wished for liberty. Wherefore, he admonished them, that they should be wise and after the manner of a good husbandman that tilled his ground, and did cut away all noisome weeds that were accustomed to grow and oppress the fruit, that they should make haste to do now at this present the like.*
>
> *First the Archbishop and great men of the kingdom were to be slain; after, lawyers, justices, lastly whomsoever they knew like hereafter to be hurtful to the Commons, they should dispatch out of the land, for so might they purchase safety to themselves hereafter, if the great men being once taken away, there remained amongst them equal liberty, all one nobility, and like authority and power.*[3]

None of the peasants who heard Ball's words could have any doubt now about the seriousness of what they were doing. The 'great men' who had brought such suffering and indignity on the heads of the commons were to receive revolutionary justice. A new order was to prevail. But now to work. A section of the peasant army moved off to the meeting place that had been agreed with the royal group whilst the rest waited and prepared to take the city.

The royal barge carrying the king with his earls and ministers had left the Tower a little earlier and had headed down river to the appointed meeting place. Behind this were four more barges containing the king's knights. They were all filled with a deep

ichard ij allant à la rencontre des serfs anglais révoltés

At Greenwich the royal party made a futile attempt to negotiate with Tyler's army.

foreboding. The Earl of Salisbury expressed it well: 'If the rebels are successful . . . then . . . it will be all over with us and our heirs, and England will be a desert.'[4]

As they approached, the royal party became even more unnerved. On the bank they saw upwards of 10,000 peasants who had come to that place to meet with the king. Their appearance was not at all that of a wild and dishevelled rabble. Banners of St George and hundreds of pennants fluttered in the wind and the polished steel of swords and armour flashed in the bright June sun. On the sight of the king

and his retinue, there was a rush to the bank of the river and a great
clamour went up. The peasants were waving and shouting to Richard
to come ashore.

Observing this scene, the royal group were immediately of the
view that the king should not, under any circumstances, land. The
earls and Sudbury, who was also in the boat, were afraid for their
lives and with good reason. Already the rebels had petitioned the
king for their heads. They also feared that the king might be
captured by the rebels. The king shouted to the bank, 'Sirs, tell me
what you want.' The answer came back loud and clear: 'We wish
thee to land where we will remonstrate with thee and tell thee
more at our ease what our wants are.' There was a pause and then
the Earl of Salisbury rose to answer for the king. Nothing he said in
his reply could have better captured the absurdity of their
situation. Standing with all the rectitude of his type, he bellowed,
'Gentlemen, you are not properly dressed, nor in a fit condition
for the king to talk with you.'[5] The chronicler, Froissart, records
that no further negotiations took place and the royal barge was then
rowed hastily back up the Thames to the Tower. We can imagine
that very little was said amongst the king and his nobles either, for at
this point there was little to suggest. The rebuff, however, had
infuriated the peasants and now they determined to enter London.

Southwark, on the south side of the river, was already in peasant
hands and Tyler now led his men to the Marshalsea prison. The
freeing of prisoners at Southwark, and earlier at Rochester, is a
significant theme in the revolt. It again points to the class-conscious
motives driving events forward. The prisoners were victims of the
system that the peasants opposed and their liberation was one of the
tasks the peasants set themselves. Sudbury's palace at Lambeth,
along with all legal documents found there, was also put to the
torch, as were brothels owned by the mayor of London, William
Walworth. The rebels now set out to London Bridge to gain access
to the City of London.

Both of the peasant armies were soon poised to enter the city.
Straw's army, north of the river, had moved from its Mile End
encampment to the Ald Gate. On the south bank Tyler's men had
assembled at London Bridge. The Stonegate of the bridge was its
main defence. The aldermen, who had control of access to the city,
were in an impossible position. Behind them there was a London

population who detested the royal court and supported the commons. In front of them were peasant armies who threatened to destroy the Ald Gate and London Bridge if they were not allowed to enter.

Guild rivalries also played their part at this decisive moment. The victualling guilds, especially the fishmongers and grocers, were out to establish monopolies on food imported into the city. To this end they sought favour with the king. They were led by a former mayor of London, Nicholas Bramber, and their party included William Walworth and a wool merchant, Richard Lyons. The non-victualling guilds, worried by the effect that food monopolies would have on prices and their own trades, opposed them and in so doing also opposed the king. They were led by John of Northampton. Thus the aldermen of the city were politically divided when the armies of Tyler and Straw arrived at the city gates.[6] There is even some evidence of prior contact between some of the aldermen and the insurgents. We know, for example, that Alderman John Horne met Wat Tyler to inform him that the city would rise to support him and that he should advance without delay. There may also have been communications some time before this. Certainly, despite Mayor Walworth's instructions to the contrary, the Ald Gate was left open to the rebels by Alderman William Tonge. At London Bridge, Ward Alderman William Sibley, having sent away those who came to defend the bridge, lowered the drawbridge to the rebels.

And so, on 13 June the peasants entered London as a conquering army. They marched with discipline. Each section represented a town or village. One hundred here for a town, twenty or so there for a small village and so on. Altogether perhaps 60,000 peasants were now in occupation of the city.[7] The orderly fashion with which they conducted themselves reflected their clarity of purpose. They had already declared that there would be no wild rampage. The Londoners were not their enemies. Indeed, the peasants had even promised to pay for all of the food and drink they were afforded by the London populace, who welcomed them so warmly into the city. Some had put word about that these peasants were devils who would carry out murder and burn homes indiscriminately. There have been historians who have written as though this was what the peasants intended. But is it not so often the case that two groups of people, so long separated by their oppressors, find, on their meeting, that they are remarkably alike, that they have much in common, and that given the choice they would far rather join with each other than with their rulers? But there were some in the city whose property and persons were now at the mercy of those whom they had treated for so long with contempt.

The peasants now broke up into different sections, dispatched to different parts of the city. Whilst the largest group set off to the Strand to find the Savoy, the palace of John of Gaunt, another group went further west. There was no wanton destruction of property on their way to their appointed destinations. Only when they reached the Fleet did the attacks begin. First the Fleet prison was besieged to free the prisoners there. The houses and shops of the wealthy were then destroyed. The peasants now made for the Temple, the lawyers' quarter of the city.

The attack on the lawyers' quarter is again, as with almost every aspect of the actions of the peasants in London, highly significant. It was here that the feudal laws of England were devised and protected. Here were the people who created the legal edifice of bondage, of land ownership and of tribute. These lawyers provided the framework within which the oppression of the villein occurred. The daily robbery of labour and goods and the constant humiliations that made up the life of the villein were given legitimation by the work of these men. They were high on the rebels' list of enemies of the commons. The lawyers themselves got off relatively lightly or simply escaped, but the Temple was razed to the ground. A bonfire was made of all parchments, documents, legal records and so on. The laws of feudalism were burned to ash.

Next on the peasants' route were the houses of a religious order, the Hospital of St John. The hated Robert Hales was head of the Knights of St John and so its buildings were burned. The London crowd cheered on the attack and insisted that they had been going to do the very same thing only two years before.[8] Now these rebels went on to join those who had gone ahead for the greatest prize of all, the Savoy. The temptation merely to sack the Savoy for booty may have been present in the minds of some of the rebels. It was a truly sumptuous place which John of Gaunt had only just had finished. It was decorated in the very latest finery and was a treasure trove that rivalled the wealth of the king himself. To the rebels it must have seemed like something from another world, which in a sense, of course, it was. Wat Tyler, however, had given strict instruction that there would be no looting for personal gain:

> *none, on pain to lose his head, should presume to convert to his*
> *own use anything that there was or might be found, but that*
> *they should break such plate and vessels of gold and silver, as*
> *were in that house in great plenty, into small pieces, and throw*
> *the same into the Thames or into privies. Clothes of gold and*
> *silver and silk and velvet, they should tear; rings and jewels set*
> *with precious stones they should break into mortars, that the*
> *same might be of no use.*[9]

One man who did not understand the seriousness of Tyler's word on this matter and who tried to filch a silver plate for himself was thrown into the flames of the burning palace. There were some who drank themselves stupid in the duke's wine cellars and so also perished in the flames. Tyler was insistent that they would not be called robbers by those who sought to discredit them. This was not a grubby enterprise driven by envy or personal greed. Their aim was the destruction of feudalism. And so they set about the systematic destruction of the palace of the most hated man in England with an almost detached and methodical calmness. Everything was to be committed to the flames:

> *they took all the torches they could find, and lighted them, and*
> *burnt all the sheets and coverlets and beds and headboards of*
> *great worth, for their whole value was estimated at 1,000*
> *marks. And all the napery and other things that they could*
> *discover they carried to the hall and set on fire with their*
> *torches. And they burnt the hall, and the chambers, and all the*
> *buildings within the gates of the said palace or manor, which*
> *the commons of London had left unburnt. And, as is said, they*
> *found three barrels of gunpowder, and thought it was gold or*
> *silver, and cast it into the fire, and the powder exploded, and set*
> *the hall in a greater blaze than before, to the great loss and*
> *damage of the Duke of Lancaster.*[10]

It was fortunate for Gaunt that he was not himself in London at this time. There is no question that he would have died at the hands of the peasants. He was with his army fighting on the Scottish border and on hearing the news of events in London was in no haste to return. But by the complete destruction of the Savoy, the symbol of his prestige, the rebels had dealt him a humiliating blow and had in effect put an end to his ambitions for the throne. They moved on now, along the Strand, to Westminster. The Westminster prison was attacked and the prisoners were released. They went next along Holborn to the Newgate prison and again freed those inside. All the way they attacked and burned down the properties of those whom they identified as enemies and traitors. Eventually they arrived at St Martins-le-Grand, where they found one Roger Legett, a notorious magistrate who had inflicted feudal punishment on many a poor wretch. He was dragged from the church where he had been praying for his life and beheaded. The *Chronicle Anonimalle* records that eighteen other heads were taken on this day of justice, to be displayed on London Bridge.

On the night of 13 June the fires of London lit up the night sky. From where he stood on the balcony of the Tower, Richard could see the flames leaping from the Savoy and the red, smoke-filled sky over the city. At the bottom of the Tower, a large number of the peasant army were now encamped to ensure that none could escape from that fortress without being seen. Richard and his advisers considered their position. There had only been three royal armies in England on the outbreak of the rising. One was with Gaunt in the north and one in Wales with the Earl of Buckingham, recently returned exhausted from his disastrous campaign in France. The third was with the Earl of Cambridge at Plymouth and Dartmouth, ready for embarkation to Spain and waiting for better weather to sail. As news came of events around London, the gallant earl surmised that it might be better to leave for Spain without delay – which is exactly what he did.

As he gazed out over the city of London, ablaze in every direction, the enormity of what had occurred must have weighed heavily on Richard. The rebels were in complete control of London and the royal party were utterly defenceless. Of course, the Tower could not be taken without a serious siege and they could survive behind its walls for a long time. But could they win back control of the city?

Their fate, in terms of their power and wealth, and indeed in terms of their very lives, hung by a thread. The king sought the counsel of his advisers.

As the earls discussed their situation, two schools of opinion emerged. Walworth, mayor of London, still in a state of indignant fury at the destruction of his precious brothels on the south side of the river, was for drowning the rebels in blood. Excitedly, he pressed his argument. The rebels were asleep and those who were not were drunk. A disciplined body of men could break into their ranks and kill enough of them to disorientate the rest. The Earl of Salisbury, the most experienced of the nobles around the king and a military man, disagreed. With the majority of the Londoners supporting the rebels, how could they be sure of success? If they embarked on such a course of action without success, it would deepen the crisis. As he put it: 'If we commence a thing we can't carry through, we're done for.'[11] Salisbury had a different plan. They had no choice, he argued, but to make concessions and if necessary to concede everything in order to get the peasants to disperse. Better to use guile in an attempt to divide the most revolutionary of the rebels from the rest.

Their cunning was born of the desperate position that they were in. But there was one fact that made the nobles believe that they might succeed. There was no question that the rebels hated every one of them and that, if they kept control of London, the royal group would lose their lives. There was one, however, in whom the rebels had trust – the king himself. The cry of the rebels had not gone unnoticed – for King Richard and the True Commons. The nobles must have wondered how such an unlikely person as this could be held in such affection by the people:

> *Neither by natural disposition nor youthful training was he fitted to come through the troubles bequeathed to him by his grandfather. Abrupt and stammering in speech, hasty and subject to sudden gusts of passion . . . the somewhat unmanly despair attributed to him . . . may not be out of keeping with his character.*[12]

And yet this boy, it seemed, too young to have blood on his hands or to have become the detested figure that he would become in later life, might be the nobles' salvation.

They now began to push Richard into the foreground of their plan. Richard was sent with a statement for the commons. He stood at the east-facing St Catherine's Tower and passed down a statement that was read out by a sergeant at arms standing on a chair to be heard. The statement promised immunity to all the rebels as long as they dispersed and returned to their villages:

> *The king thanks his good commons for their loyalty and pardons all their illegal offences, but he wishes everyone to return home and set down his grievance in writing and send it to him. By the advice of his lords he will then provide such remedy as will be profitable to himself, his commons and the whole realm.*[13]

The shallowness of this gesture after such dramatic events offended the rebels and they shouted back that such a response was nothing but an insult. They would not be made fools of and some set off immediately to finish work they felt had not been done well enough at the Temple. The rejection of this first attempt at conciliation by the king was a salutary lesson to the group in the Tower. This would not be an easy night. These serfs had not come this far only to go home empty handed on some faint promise of a pardon. The earls had hoped that the peasants were the simple and gullible men they had always assumed them to be. Clearly they were not. The king and his group were obviously going to have to go much further in their attempts to negotiate with the commons of England.

Another meeting occurred on the night of 13 June. But the mood at this meeting was very different. Tyler had met with the other leaders at the house of Thomas Farringdon, an ally of the Essex army who had accompanied them through the Ald Gate. Here they discussed their advantage and the demands they would put to the king. They came to four and represented a fundamental attack on the very social relations of the feudal order. These were the demands:

1. That each man should be beholden only to himself and that no man should be bonded to his lord.

2. That none of the rebels should be punished for their actions in the rising for they acted in the name of justice and right was on their side.
3. That the peasant be granted the right to sell his produce in the fairs and markets and whichever town and borough he chose.
4. That land rent should be set at 4d an acre.

They wanted an end to the unfree status of the villein. Implicit in this was a call for an end to the Statute of Labourers, since it meant that the relationship between a lord and his labourers should be subject to contract. It was an economic demand because it meant that the peasant could leave the manor to which he was bonded and go to labour on the demesne of another lord. It was also a cry for personal freedom and an end to the humiliation of lordly domination.

The rebels wanted immunity from punishment, of course – a demand that must flow from the king's acceptance of the other demands.

They also wanted the right to trade on the open market. This third demand makes clear the historical cusp on which the revolution turned. Under the manorial system, the produce of the peasant went to the lord's table. If produce were sold beyond the boundaries of the manor, the lord would lose control of the primary means of feudal exploitation. It was this conflict, between the desire of the peasant to buy and sell freely and the lord's need to retain control of peasant production, which was holding back the development of the market in English society. It was not only the peasants who railed against this restriction on their commercial activity, but also the burghers of the towns and cities that were pushing for independence from the crown and also many of the London guilds that were seeking more freedom to trade beyond London. It was in this sense that the social relations upon which the feudal order rested were acting as a fetter on the development of a new economic and social order. They were holding back the development of capitalism.

The final demand was significant in that it proposed a universal rent that would apply everywhere in the kingdom. As the wages of peasant labourers rose with demand after the Black Death, the feudal state hit back in ways we have already described. On a local level, lords had tried to make their villeins pay for the increased labour costs by raising land rents and other dues. There was tremendous unevenness in what a peasant might have to pay from one part of the country to another. In some areas, serfs paid almost 2 shillings an acre. In demanding the lowest rent for the whole country, the rebels again demonstrated that they were not simply thinking of personal gain. They were concerned first and foremost to promote a practical plan for a new way of organizing society. That vision, which had inspired the leaders and followers of the Great Society, was no longer just a distant notion. The dream, so it seemed, was becoming real.

The king agreed to meet with the rebel leaders the following morning at Mile End, outside the walls of the city. This meeting actually posed something of a dilemma for the rebel leaders. There was no question that a large number of their followers, perhaps the majority, had a naïve understanding of the king's sympathy for their cause. They believed that the king was their friend. Tyler and the other leaders, however, had a far more clear-sighted view of what the king represented and the way in which the nobles controlled him. They noted in particular that the king had called on the peasants to rally at Mile End over the heads of the leaders.

On the other hand, the rebels were in an enormously powerful position. This was their hour and the king was in their hands. It was the rebels' intention then to capture the king, certainly in the political sense of using his name to legitimize their demands, and possibly even literally. From the confession of Jack Straw before his execution, it seems that the rebels considered the possibility of holding the king and taking him around the country to give his authority to charters of freedom for each town and village and to manumissions from serfdom. This was an entirely plausible plan. There is no question that the king's word and even the king's presence with the rebels in each county would have gone a long way to overcoming opposition from local gentry and would have made their plan for the abolition of serfdom a great deal easier.

By the following morning around 100,000 serfs and Londoners had gathered at Mile End. In the fourteenth century Mile End was a small village surrounded by open spaces, allowing this huge assembly to occur. The meeting had been set for 7 a.m. As the king and his group approached Mile End on horseback, peasants on either side of them began shouting out their demands and grievances. As the commotion rose, the royal entourage became agitated. The king himself was not at all the heroic figure that some historians have made him out to be. Chronicles of the time record that he was visibly nervous. As the pressure increased, two of the lords, the Duke of Kent and Sir Thomas Holland, suddenly broke ranks and galloped across the open fields towards Whitechapel to save their own skins. When the king moved forward, petitioning hands grabbed at the reigns of his horse. At one point Thomas Farringdon intercepted the king to request the head of the traitor Hales. The king replied that they 'might work their will on any traitors who could be proved such by law'.[14] In doing this Richard knew that he was condemning Hales and Sudbury, who had been left behind in the Tower, to death. Farringdon now rode off to the Tower to make sure that their quarry did not escape.

As Richard reached the meeting point, the rebel army knelt to greet the boy-king whom they believed would be their salvation. In an implicit reference to the power of John of Gaunt, they received him with the following words:

> *Welcome to our Lord King Richard, if it pleases you, and we will not have any other king but you.*[15]

Wat Tyler then proceeded to put forward the peasants' demands. Richard agreed to every single one of them. Only on one issue did the king hesitate. When Tyler demanded that all the traitors of England be seized and put to death, Richard's answer was evasive. Only when pressed by Tyler a second time did the king relent.

We can only look back with amazement that things had really come to this. The king of England was deferring to the leader of the commons of England. The authority of government was now in Tyler's hands. On 14 June 1381 the social pyramid that was the feudal order was standing on its head. This was the moment of victory and now once again there was work to be done. Thirty lawyers were brought from the Temple to Mile End and some also sent to St Paul's in the city. All day long they received delegations from every part of the country and drew up charters in the king's name. Each document was a charter of freedom granting all of the Mile End demands for even the smallest village. We still have fragments of some of these charters. Their wording was unequivocal. Here is the charter for Hertford:

> *Know that of our special grace we have manumitted all our liege and singular subjects and other of the county of Hertford, freed each and all of their old bondage, and made them quit by these presents; pardoned them all felonies, treasons and transgressions, and extortions committed by any and all of them, and assure them of our 'summa pax'.*[16]

Tyler himself now rode to the Tower to dispense justice with the king's authority. Hales and Sudbury and others of the king's familiars had been left at the Tower with a not inconsiderable guard of 600 men at arms. Unfortunately for them the opinion of the guards was ambivalent. It seems they had some sympathy with the rising. When Sudbury had tried to escape from the Tower, he was spotted by a woman who raised the alarm. The rebels under Farringdon's command, however, had also received prior warning of the escape plan. Certainly when Tyler arrived from Mile End the rebels had no difficulty entering the Tower and we are told that some fraternization, joking and 'stroking of beards' went on with the guards.

The rebels now wandered from room to room looking for the traitors. Those members of the royal group who had remained were entirely at the mercy of the rebels. But again Tyler's men were discriminating. John of Gaunt's young son was spared, for example, although William Appleton, his physician and adviser, was beheaded. The king's mother had her second scare of the week when the rebels entered her bedchamber and again after some jocularities – one of the peasants, it seems, tried to give her a kiss – was left alone. John Legge, the deviser of the third poll tax, went to the block. Hales and Sudbury had been preparing for death in the Tower chapel from soon after the king's departure. Their escape plan had not succeeded and, although the Tower was a rabbit warren of secret passages and hiding places, they knew that they could not trust the guards not to have given them away. They awaited their fate with a certain stoicism. When the rebels burst in, Sudbury managed some words of protest but the two were unceremoniously bustled out to Tower Hill by the rebels:

There they cut off the heads of Master Simon Sudbury, Archbishop of Canterbury, and of Sir Robert Hales, Prior of the Hospital of St John's, Treasurer of England, and of Sir William Appleton, a great lawyer and surgeon, and one who had much power with the king and the Duke of Lancaster. [17]

The heads were displayed on London Bridge in a manner which suggests that the rebels saw themselves acting in the king's name. This had, after all, been the traditional fate of traitors to England. Sudbury also suffered the eternal indignity of having his mitre attached to his head with a nail to keep it from falling off.

Retribution at the hands of the commons was by now sweeping all over London. Richard Lyons, the most important merchant in London and one who had opposed the Good Parliament, was beheaded at Cheapside. The lawyers who had escaped the previous day were not so lucky now. Tax collectors too were targeted, as were profiteers and unjust landlords. The objects of popular indignation and punishment were sometimes pointed out by the Londoners who knew them well and, of course, we cannot completely rule out the occurrence of revenge of a more personal nature amidst these events.

The ugliest aspect of the events of 14 June, and one which best illustrates the separate agenda of the Londoners, was the massacre of the Flemings. It was Edward III who had brought the Flemish weavers to England to develop the textile industry. They operated as a society within a society with their own guilds, servants, customs and rituals. They had long aroused the resentment of the other London guilds and some of the Londoners now saw the opportunity to settle old scores. And so the old cry went up – 'the foreigners are to blame for our woes'. It was as untrue then as it is now. Nonetheless any revolution is the product of the society from which it has arisen and it is possible for negative features to emerge within events that we otherwise celebrate. What we can say with confidence is that this had nothing to do with Tyler's army. The peasants of Essex and Kent and the other counties had no quarrel with, indeed little knowledge of, the Flemings. In fact, the leader of the Yarmouth rebels was himself Flemish. But equally, no honest history can pass over this event. It is a salutary reminder of the importance of the highest levels of consciousness in the revolutionary process.

Whilst the rebels took their revenge on those who had oppressed them for so long, the survivors of the royal group were reassembling at the Wardrobe – a fortified building in Carter Lane near the Lud Gate. The king's mother had already gone there to seek the refuge she so badly needed. It was impossible for the king to go back to the Tower following the executions there earlier in the day. He was forced instead, extraordinary as it seems, to make his own way with a small number of his party to the Wardrobe. He must have witnessed, at much closer hand than had been the case so far, the real meaning of the rebels' control of London. At this point he could have been forgiven for giving all up as lost. As the king and his advisers gathered at Carter Lane, however, Salisbury's plan was taking effect.

As each of the village and town delegations had received their charters of freedom they had begun to pack up and begin the long walk back to their homes. The call of the peasant to his land is a strong one. The fields were being neglected and, anyway, the paper in their hands that said they were free carried the king's seal. They were anxious to return and resume their lives as free men and women. Generally the peasants who thought in this way were from the least economically developed areas, especially Essex. The 30,000 or so peasants who remained were mainly, though not exclusively, from Kent, where there had been a much higher proportion of peasants who were already free. For them the rising had been about more than simply an end to villeinage. They were concerned with greater freedoms and their ideas went much further. It was amongst such men that Ball's egalitarian ideas held sway and from whom calls came for the property of the Church to be taken from it and distributed to the poor. Nonetheless, a division was opening up between the most advanced and leading elements of the rising and the peasants who did not think much further than their fields. This division was, of course, to nobody's advantage but the king's.

Wat Tyler requested a second meeting with the king, this time at Smithfield. The clique around the king at Carter Lane was plotting again, but now with murderous intent. They sent word through John Newton that the king would meet Tyler that evening. At about three they set out from the Wardrobe and first of all went westward to Westminster Abbey. Here they took absolution and it is said that they prayed fervently. Richard himself prayed for over an hour with one of the friars, seeking assurance that what he was about to do was no sin. As they rode away from the abbey, their appearance belied their true purpose, for their robes concealed the armour they wore underneath.

Smithfield was the site of the city's cattle fair and its soil stank with the blood of slaughter. On arriving there the king and his group saw the massed ranks of the remaining rebels, still around 30,000 in number. These were also the most determined of the rebels and the sight of them must have been daunting. After taking up their position on the far side of the fields, away from Tyler's army, the royal party sent Walworth over to the rebels to request that Tyler accompany him to meet with the king. It shows Tyler's confidence at this moment that he agreed to go with Walworth with only two or three attendants and armed only with a dagger. Tyler felt in command of the situation and so went, almost completely undefended, to the vipers' nest.

On meeting Richard, Tyler stepped down from his horse, knelt before the king and, holding his hand warmly, pledged to him the loyalty of the commons. He now rose to present the king with a new set of demands. These went further than the demands that had been put only the previous day at Mile End and reveal the true radicalism that inspired the most far seeing of the rebels:

> *Let no law but the law of Winchester prevail, and let no man be made an outlaw by the decree of judges and lawyers. No lord shall exercise lordship over the Commons; and since we are oppressed by so vast a hoard of bishops and clerks let there be but one bishop in England. The property and the goods of the holy church should be taken and divided according to the needs of the people in each parish, after making provision for the existing clergy and monks, and finally let there be no more villeins in England, but all to be free and of one condition.*[18]

This appeal for the 'law of Winchester' to be restored referred back to the Statute of Winchester that had been passed by Edward I. It had established a system of governance based on localities and upon an armed population. It had been passed before the emergence of the much more bureaucratic and centralized state of the later fourteenth century. The demand for Winchester law to be restored essentially meant the repeal of all the legislation that had been passed since the Black Death of 1348 and which had been designed to push back the English peasantry into a cowed and subservient position. Similarly, the demand that the status of 'outlaw' be abolished hit at the oppressive legal apparatus of the feudal state. To be an outlaw in England meant being completely outside of society. The outlaw could possess no property, had no legal rights or protection and could be lawfully killed by anyone. The status of outlaw had been falling into disuse but had been revived as a means of imposing the Statute of Labourers. The demands for the end of lordship and villeinage were a restatement of the appeal for personal freedom and the ending of serfdom that had been put to the king the previous day. The power and wealth of the manor was to be pared down to 'narrow proportions, as between man and man, excepting our lord the king'.[19] The lords would remain such in name only.

A wholly new demand was that for the stripping away of the wealth of the Church and its distribution to the commons. It may have always been the intention of the revolutionaries to put this demand, but certainly the events of the previous 48 hours must have emboldened them. Their assault on the power of the clergy was thoroughly revolutionary. There would be only one bishop in England. This would have been, of course, John Ball. The vast areas of land owned by the Church would be distributed to the commons. The ordinary parish priests would be maintained, but the wealthy priests, bishops, abbots and friars of the religious orders would lose their privilege and wealth. When we remember the economic as well as ideological power that the Church wielded in the medieval world, the impact of such ideas was earthshaking. These demands had come up from those who had been the poorest and most downtrodden section of society, but who now stood before their king as free men and women – the 'True Commons'. The king, according to the plan devised by Salisbury, conceded every one of the demands put to him.

Tyler, happy but exhausted, now called for beer to wet his throat and toast the new order of things. The onlooking nobles bristled with irritation at the familiarity of this upstart with the king. They now moved to make their kill. A page had been primed to goad Tyler. He shouted out that he knew Tyler to be a rogue and a thief.

**With Tyler mortally wounded, the king appeals to the peasants
to end the rising and return to their fields.**

Tyler, now back on his horse, span around at this impudence to see
who it was who had spoken. The page was pushed forward to repeat
his accusation. The furious Tyler ordered one of his attendants to
dismount and behead the page and, sensing the sudden change in
atmosphere, drew his own dagger. The drawing of Tyler's dagger in
the king's presence was the pretext the nobles had been waiting for.
They descended on him now like hounds. Walworth stabbed Tyler
in the head and neck as Tyler struck back only to find his weapon
hitting the steel armour beneath Walworth's robes. The other
nobles, particularly Ralph Standiche and John Cavendish, were now
stabbing wildly. The rebel army across the fields could not see
properly what was happening. On seeing the flash of steel, some
thought that their leader was being knighted. But when Tyler's
horse broke away from the band of murderers around the king with
the dying Tyler lying across it, they realized what had happened.

There are moments when history turns on the point of a needle
and this was such a moment. The rebels, on seeing Tyler fall from

his horse and outraged at what had occurred, began to bend their bows to the sky. The longbows that had brought victories to the English armies at Crécy and Poitiers were now turned against the rulers of England. In the next moment, arrows were about to rain down on the king and his nobles. They would have been killed and the outcome of the revolt would have been very different indeed. But now Richard made a frenzied gallop across the fields to where the rebels stood and cried out that they should trust him. The fact that Richard was alone, the brave nobles having abandoned him as they scattered for their lives, must have made Richard's appeal more convincing. But, more importantly, it was in the young king that they had invested their hopes. They had their charters of freedom in their hands and now they had the king's word that these charters would be honoured. Bewildered at the loss of their leader, they listened to Richard and began to move towards Clerkenwell fields from thence to disperse and go home.

False victory! They had been tricked and they did not yet know it. They were soon to learn a lesson that every generation of the oppressed and exploited learns in their own way – that the cowardice and deceit of the ruling class, of any ruling class, knows no limit. They will sacrifice their own and they will scrape the ground in their assurances that they can be trusted and that they have honour. They have no honour and they flatter in order to deceive. As Richard conceded the demands at Smithfield, the sword that would strike the rebels down when they did not expect it had already been unsheathed. Sir Robert Knowles had mustered a force of perhaps 8,000 since the executions at the Tower, when even those wealthy citizens who had originally seen some advantage to themselves in the rising had realized their real class interests and had decided that things had already gone too far. They now appeared and would have attacked the disoriented rebels if it had not been for the king. Sensing that the situation was still dangerous, he stayed Knowles' hand and allowed the rebels to go. Retribution would follow when Tyler's army was more dispersed.

Tyler, mortally wounded, had been taken to the hospital at St Bartholomew's. Walworth hunted him down there a short time later and, after dragging the bleeding Tyler on to the grounds of the hospital, had him beheaded. He who had raised his people from the indignity of serfdom to look their rulers square in the eye was not afforded the right to a dignified death. Tyler's murderers got their reward. Walworth – the brothel-keeper mayor – was knighted by the king at Smithfield. Ralph Standiche was later made constable of York. The celebration of the ruling class at the killing of Tyler remains to this day. A glance at the coat of arms of the City of London shows it, for in the upper right-hand quarter of the shield of St George is an upward-pointing dagger. This was to become a symbol of the murder of Tyler at Walworth's hand.

But Tyler's was the real reward. His name still rings down the centuries as a warning to those who oppress and as a clarion call to those who are oppressed. His name is for ever associated with the cause of freedom and that is an honour worth more than any gold or title.

The back of the peasants' revolt in London had been broken. But our story is not yet finished, for around the country the rising was still in full flow. It is to events outside London that we must now turn.

CHAPTER 5

REPRESSION AND CONTINUING REVOLT

As news of Tyler's success in London and stories of the charters of freedom issued at Mile End spread beyond London, the surrounding shires rose up to join the revolt. Over 13 and 14 June, the high point of the rebels' control of London, risings began also at Bury, St Albans and Cambridge. On 16 June the rising in East Suffolk began, and it spread to West Suffolk the following day. Although Kent, Essex and London had been the storm centre of the revolt, its ripples spread as far as York and Scarborough, with final echoes being heard even as far away as the Wirral.

The leader of the revolt in the East Anglian counties was John Wraw. Wraw had been in London and in communication with Wat Tyler and other leading figures of the Kent and Essex armies when they had occupied the city. Now he returned to take the revolt to the outlying regions. On 12 June, Wraw led his forces from the Essex town of Liston to Overhall, where they sacked the home of Richard Lyons, who would be executed by the London rebels two days later. They then proceeded to the town of Cavendish on the Suffolk border to raid the property of the king's justice and local enforcer of the Statute of Labourers, the hated John de Cavendish. After fortifying themselves at the tavern of a certain Onewene of Melford, they set out to take the Suffolk capital of Bury St Edmunds.

At Bury, Wraw and his followers now sacked the house of the prior and the town house of John de Cavendish. Cavendish himself had fled. He was pursued through the parish of Lakenheath. Rushing along the river bank there, he had spied a boat with which he hoped to make good his get away. His hopes were frustrated, however, by one Katherine Gamen, who, standing near to the boat, observed Cavendish heading towards her with the rebels in hot pursuit. After a moment's reflection Katherine turned and pushed it firmly out into the river. Cavendish was swiftly caught and promptly beheaded. Thus did Katherine Gamen of Lakenheath earn her place in the people's history of England!

Another hated figure in the town was the prior of the abbey, John de Cambridge. The town had long known tension between the abbey and the populace. The prior knew that to stay in the town was very dangerous for him and that fleeing was his only chance of surviving the town rising. He also was apprehended, however, on the word of a disloyal guide. Shortly after, he too was executed and his head displayed alongside that of his old friend Cavendish. The rebels made jest of the men who for too long had oppressed them, positioning their heads, first one whispering into the other's ear in confession, and then with kissing lips. The sacking of the homes of the wealthy and general rioting continued over several days. At every turn the manorial rolls were burned and with them centuries of feudal bondage. In the midst of these events Mettingham Castle was taken by Wraw's army on 19 June.

In Norfolk events were also proceeding apace. The leadership there consisted principally of the dyer, Geoffrey Litster, and, as his lieutenant, the knight, Sir Roger Bacon. Litster mustered his forces at Mousehold Heath[1] on 17 June. In great numbers the rebels now marched to the city walls of Norwich and demanded that the constable of the city, Robert Salle, come and speak to them. Salle was a figure who had come from humble beginnings, having himself been a bondsman, and had risen through military service to a position of considerable status and wealth. True to his breed, he had a haughty contempt for the background he had left behind and was certainly not about to bow to those whom he viewed as his social inferiors. He came out of the city walls to meet with the rebels, but he would not comply with their demand that he join them. After a struggle he paid for his high-handed behaviour towards the peasants with his life.

On seeing the death of Salle, the town burgesses put up no further resistance to Litster and he proceeded to occupy the city of Norwich. Taking up residence in Norwich Castle, Litster now set about spreading the revolt to all of the surrounding districts and adjudicating over disputes and matters brought to him by the people of the region. Again, manorial rolls all over the area were sought out and destroyed. The riches of the local gentry and nobility were taken to Norwich Castle, from where they would later be used by Litster in an attempt to buy the freedom of the city. For six days Litster was in effective control of Norwich and its environs, earning the title 'King of the Commons' from his supporters – a title enhanced by his insistence that the captured lords of the region wait on him at his table.

Whilst Suffolk and Norfolk were ablaze, dramatic events were also unfolding in Cambridge. In the wider county, rioting had been occurring even since 9 June. Communications had been going on between the rebel leadership in London and the insurgents of Cambridgeshire. By 15 June, however, the revolt was in full flow. In all parts of Cambridgeshire, manor houses, abbeys and the estates of the famously rich and powerful were sacked and plundered, and the documents of feudal repression destroyed. In Cambridge itself, tensions between the town and the political power of the university provided a rich seam of local antagonism. There had already been disturbances in April of that year. Now with the revolt in full throttle, violence erupted once again. From 15 to 17 June the rebels had complete control of the city. The homes of all those associated with the implementation of the statutes or the poll tax were attacked. The college and hospital of Corpus Christi were attacked and ransacked, and the university's title and property deeds destroyed.

The rebel leaders now drew up a new charter to which the university was made to submit. It stripped the university of its old privileges and powers. The university's courts were abolished so that town folk would now have their cases heard in the borough courts. A bond of £3,000 was exacted in order to protect the inhabitants of the town against any attempt by the university authorities to obtain damages for the actions of the rebels.

According to the assizes that were written after the repression of the revolt, the rebels surrounded the mayor of the town and instructed him thus:

> *You are the mayor of this the King's town and governor of our community, if you do not consent to our will and commands and carrying out all that shall be said to you on behalf of the King and his faithful Commons, you will be at once beheaded.*[2]

The mayor, Edmund Redmeadow, duly complied and became the reluctant 'leader' of an attack upon the local priory. There had been a long-standing feud between local people and the prior over access to pasturage on priory land, the prior having effectively enclosed his fields. The rebels now set about the priory buildings:

> *They marched out over 1,000 strong by Barnwell Causeway, and fell upon the priory, pulling down walls and felling trees to the value of £400, draining fish ponds, and carrying off turfs for the winter. The enclosures round the Estenhall meadows were, of course, obliterated to the last stake.*[3]

Despite this wave of revolt spreading outwards from the south-east, however, the counter-offensive of the ruling group around the king was already in full swing. On 15 June, Walworth had presented King Richard with the head of Wat Tyler. Richard now granted dictatorial powers to Walworth to win back control of London. Walworth was invested with the authority to dispense retribution for the impudence of the peasants, either within the law or 'by other ways and means'. If the rebels who had followed Tyler and Straw had any lingering illusions in the king as their friend, they were soon to be dispelled by the beheadings, torture and mutilation that characterized Walworth's Terror in London over the months of July and August. The tide had turned and was running powerfully against the rebels.

The leading figures of the revolt were now being rounded up and made to suffer Walworth's revenge. Jack Straw was an early victim. Before he was executed, he made a 'confession' that reveals a great deal about the intentions of the rebels. We have already had cause to mention Tyler's plan to take the young King Richard around England to use his authority to manumit villeinage in every region. Straw tells us, however, that it was also the intention of the rebel leadership to arrest and execute the wealthiest men in the land and to expropriate all the property of the Church. With the exception of the mendicant orders, the entire clerical hierarchy was to be abolished. England was to become a federation of self-governing communes. In the end, the king would have been executed and 'when there was no one greater or stronger or more learned than ourselves surviving, we would have made such laws as pleased us'.[4]

As the repression continued, the influence of class was apparent.

Those figures amongst the rebels who were of the gentry were punished differently from those who were of the people. Thomas Farringdon, for example, who had taken the Tower and overseen the executions of Sudbury and Hales, was imprisoned but escaped execution. The aldermen who had allowed the peasant armies to enter the city were released on bail. Those greater and lesser leaders who were peasants themselves, or at least were not of high birth, aroused the greatest fear and loathing in their tormentors and were without exception sent to their deaths.

On 18 June a proclamation was made charging all sheriffs with responsibility for the punishment of rebels in their areas and with running down any rebels who were in hiding. On 20 June, Sir Thomas Trivet, constable of the castle at Dover, was charged with the pacification of Kent. The Earl of Suffolk, William Ufford, was dispatched to his county with 500 lances. It was in Essex, however, that the revolt was still rumbling. King Richard led his army there on 22 June and stopped at Waltham. Here a delegation of peasants from Essex came to speak to Richard to ask that he honour the promises that he himself had made to them regarding their freedom, and also to request that they no longer be obliged to attend the king's courts. Richard's answer expressed all the contempt, then and now, of the rich for the poor. In the same way that the words of John Ball ring down to us over the centuries as a clarion call of freedom, so do Richard's words ring down to us as a warning to all who suffer the delusion that there are 'friends of the people' amongst the rich and powerful in society. Coldly eyeing the peasants kneeling before him, he uttered these words:

> *O most vile and odious by land and sea, you who are not worthy to live when compared with the lords whom ye have attacked; you should be forthwith punished with vilest deaths were it not for the office ye bear. Go back to your comrades and bear the king's answer. You were and are serfs, and shall remain in bondage, not that of old, but in one infinitely worse, more vile without comparison. For as long as we live, and by God's help rule over this realm, we shall attempt by all our faculties, powers, and means to make you such an example of offence to the heirs of your servitude as that they may have you before their eyes, as in a mirror, and you may supply them with a*

> *perpetual ground for cursing and fearing you, and fear to commit the like.*[5]

The delegation who had heard these words reported to the waiting rebels of Essex. On hearing what had been said, they realized that they had two options. They could surrender and prostrate themselves at the mercy of the king or they could refuse to bow and so fight to defend their newly won freedom, even at the risk of their lives. They chose the latter course. The rebels gathered at Billericay. Reinforcements came from Great Baddow and Rettenden, south of Chelmsford. They chained carts together and dug ditches to provide a strong defensive position. They were ill armed, however, and no match for a disciplined fighting force.

On 28 June, Richard sent a large cavalry of heavily armoured soldiers against the rebels and they were routed in a short time. Five hundred died at Billericay and yet the rebels fought on. They retreated to Colchester and Huntingdon, where they attempted to rally the townsfolk. But news of the death of Tyler and the repression in London had dampened the tinder that had originally ignited the revolt. The Essex rebels hoped to join forces with Wraw's army in Suffolk but unbeknown to them Wraw had already been defeated. Richard pursued them into Colchester where, on 2 July, he issued a proclamation revoking all of the promises he had made at Mile End, as well as all of the manumissions conceded as a result of the revolt.

In other parts of the country, the repression continued. From Norwich, Litster had sent an 'embassy' of three of his lieutenants, Trunch, Skeet and Kybett, to try to meet with the king and buy the freedom of the city of Norwich. However, at Icklingham on 22 June they were intercepted by the soldier-priest, Bishop Despenser. Travelling with his murderous band, Despenser had first heard of the rebellion on his estates at Peterborough. He had proceeded to that town and put down the rebels by force before moving on to Ely and Cambridge to do the same in those towns. On encountering Litster's delegation, Despenser had them beheaded and now set off in the direction of Norwich.

Litster had moved his forces out of Norwich to North Walsham and fortified his position. Despenser reoccupied the city of Norwich and then moved forward to take up the attack. There followed a swift battle that saw Litster's men massacred. Litster himself was condemned to be hanged by the bishop. Despenser then, having carried out one atrocity after another, suddenly decided that Litster was entitled to a Christian confession before his death. The fate of Litster's soul, it seems, was of concern to the bishop, who heard his confession himself and granted him absolution. He then, it is said, supported Litster's head whilst he was dragged to the gallows, so that it would not be dashed against the cobblestones. It is in acts such as these that our oppressors sometimes betray a guilty respect for people whom they know, deep down, to be better than themselves.

The judge appointed by Richard as his Lord Chief Justice to exact punishment from the rebels was Robert Tressilian. Tressilian was notorious for his harshness and he did not disappoint his paymasters now. Every accused person brought before him was condemned and swiftly dispatched at the gallows or the block. So zealous was he in his given task that sometimes nine or ten rebels were hanged at the same time. Tressilian moved his assizes from one place to the next, and in each place that he stopped, the wealthy of the area came forward to form juries and to point the finger of accusation – and in effect of death – at whomever they chose. 1381 became remembered in popular rhymes and ballads as the year of Richard's terrible retribution against the followers of Tyler:

> *Man beware and be no fool:*
> *Think upon the axe and of the tool!*
> *The stool* [the block] *was hard, the axe was sharp,*
> *The fourth year of King Richard.*[6]

Despite the terror unleashed by the king, the bearing of the peasants was still heroic. From the records of the assizes we know that the condemned did not beg their persecutors for forgiveness, but rather stood by their actions to the last.[7]

> *Face to face with the enemy, the rebels defied their tormentors.*
> *Standing in the dock with a horrid death awaiting them, they*
> *neither cringed nor did they beg for mercy. Proudly they had*
> *fought for their class, for justice and freedom, and as proudly*
> *did they march to their death. Of all of them, from the leaders*

> *to the humblest of the rank and file, the same story is told. John*
> *Starling, who claimed that he had executed the Archbishop, was*
> *sentenced to death. Before his murder he said that he was a*
> *proud man to have been able to execute the traitor archbishop.*[8]

In the royal reaction that followed the revolt, the chroniclers tell us that 7,000 perished by the axe and the noose. Reliable estimates since have reckoned the final toll to have been less than this – probably more in the region of 2,000. There is evidence that Richard knew not to push his revenge too far, for fear of further revolt. This figure is still many times greater than the number of people killed in the rising itself, however. We should also include the thousands imprisoned in the slow death conditions of medieval dungeons following the revolt.

The final act of the revolt took place at St Albans and it is with the Hertfordshire rebellion that we will end our story.[9] St Albans had long known tension between the town and the abbey. During the reign of Edward II, the prior had seized most of the surrounding woodland and pasture. The forests, rivers and ponds had also been taken for game for the monks' table. Even by the standards of the late fourteenth century, the abbey had maintained a peculiarly powerful position with respect to its tenants, in effect enjoying the status of a manor in its own right. According to local legend, the town had been granted its independence by King Offa. Opinion had it that the monks were in possession of this charter and kept it hidden lest they lose their power and privilege. Three times the local people had risen against the monks – in 1274, 1314 and 1326 – in the name of this charter. When agents of the Great Society brought news of the first stirrings of the revolt, the peasants of St Albans saw another opportunity to shake the abbey off their backs.

On the evening of 13 June, word arrived of Tyler's entry into London. The following morning a deputation from the town went to speak to the abbot. It was led by William Grindecobbe. Grindecobbe had himself been educated at the abbey, but had fallen foul of the monks and had been excommunicated by them. He now informed the abbot, Thomas de la Mare, a noted lawyer and brother to the speaker of Parliament, that he was acting under instruction from Tyler. The delegation was to proceed that morning, he explained, to London to swear allegiance to the 'True Commons' and to obtain the freedom of the town. They now set out on the road to London.

They entered London via Highbury and as they did so they happened across Straw and his army, burning down the home of Sir Robert Hales. After some fraternization and celebration of the events that were afoot, they carried on their way to Mile End where they knew they would find Tyler. They arrived in time to witness the meeting with the king. Soon afterwards Grindecobbe held conference with Tyler, who assured him that if the monks put up resistance against the king's charter of freedom, he would send 20,000 men to 'shave the monks' beards'. Grindecobbe now left the bulk of his delegation to wait for the charters of freedom for their town and its surrounding areas. Grindecobbe himself set off with a smaller group back towards St Albans to bring the news of freedom. He arrived in St Albans that evening, having travelled 30 miles since the early morning. A great crowd had gathered to hear what he had to say:

> *That evening in torchlight perhaps, the old market lit also from open windows – for who would grudge even wax on such a night? – was one of which it is pleasant to look back, even when we know the bloody sequel. For a brief time these men and women believed that they were free. Chains were soon to follow, death was to come to many, but even while they suffered, in their heart must have remained the memory of that moment when Grindecobbe cried the news of freedom, of freedom from villein's chain, of freedom to hunt, to fish, to pasture their cattle, of freedom to grind their own corn.* [10]

The next day the townsfolk asserted their newly won freedom. Joined by rebels from Barnet, they tore down the hedges and fences with which the monks had enclosed the fields, they drained the abbot's fishpond and they divided the abbey's land between themselves. A rabbit was speared and displayed on a pole to mark the abolition of the game laws. The millstones, which had been confiscated by a previous prior to ensure that the local people paid the monks for their milling and which had been used to pave his parlour, were now dug up and returned to the families from whom they had been taken. The abbey's prison was smashed open. The rebels held an open court to re-examine the cases of the prisoners. All those prisoners who had merely fallen into debt, or who had been unable to pay the monks their fines and tithes, were released. One fellow, who was known to be an unsavoury character and who had sought the protection of the monks to save him from the wrath of the town, was found guilty of his crimes and executed.

When Grindecobbe's delegation arrived back from Mile End with the charters of freedom carrying the king's seal, Grindecobbe went again to the abbot. He demanded that the abbot now acknowledge the freedom of the town. After some attempt at legal obfuscation, the abbot consented to give a statement that recognized the new situation. Still not satisfied, the rebels withdrew to draw up their own charter which would be free of the ambiguities with which the lawyer-abbot had filled his announcement. By this time deputations were arriving from all over Hertfordshire demanding charters for their villages and all over the county the abbeys and manor homes were in flames and the local charters of bondage were being destroyed.

On 16 June, the same day that the abbot sealed the new charter drawn up by the rebels, word came that the royal army was now heading for Hertfordshire. The St Albans rebels had already heard of Tyler's murder and now they contemplated their own battle with the king. Within the royal group, however, there was also some nervousness. Anxious to avoid a battle if they could, they sent forward Sir Walter Lee, a local knight, to attempt to pacify the town. Grindecobbe agreed to meet Lee, arguing that if he had not come in peace then he would be driven from the town 'with purpose'. Lee, however, arrived with threats. He pointed out that the king's army was a short distance behind him and described also the devastation that the royal repression was bringing in its wake:

> *for miles around no fodder, nor any corn, no fruits of the earth, fresh or old are left, but all things are consumed or trodden down.*[11]

Lee now summoned a jury of twelve men whom he thought he could rely on to hand over to him the rebel leaders. The twelve, however, refused to cooperate. Frustrated, Lee resorted to cunning. In the dead of night, he and his men went to the homes of three of the rebel leaders, including Grindecobbe, and arrested them from their beds.

The next morning the townsfolk realized what had happened and prepared once more for battle. They seized their weapons, gathered in the town square and determined that they would lay siege to the abbey for the release of their leaders. The abbot, facing the destruction of his estate, got urgent word to Lee as to what was about to happen. Lee, who had been about to execute Grindecobbe and the other rebels, now realized that he had no choice but to release them. He told them to return to the town with the message that he would have a royal pardon granted if the townsfolk returned the abbey charters that they had taken, and surrendered to him. Grindecobbe returned to the town with Lee's communication and explained that if Lee's demands were not met then the rebel leaders, including himself, would be executed. Then, rising to the historical moment, Grindecobbe spoke as follows:

Fellow citizens, who now a scanty liberty has relieved from long oppression, stand while you can stand, and fear nothing for my punishment, since I would die in the cause of the liberty we have gained, if it is now my fate to die, thinking myself happy to be able to finish my life by such a martyrdom. Act now as you ought to have done if I had been executed yesterday at Hertford; for nothing would have prevented my death if the abbot had not recalled his soldiers too soon. They had indeed brought many charges against me, and they had a judge, favourable to them, and eager for my blood.[12]

There was nothing disingenuous in this. Grindecobbe had come close to death at Lee's hand the previous day and had obviously prepared himself well. His mind was clear and his words were truthful and honest. Putting aside all concern for his own fate, Grindecobbe was urging his followers to hold firm and defy the forces of reaction. Of all the moments of historical greatness that characterize the revolt, this must stand as one of the finest.

In the end, the St Albans people chose to attempt a compromise with the abbot. They may have been trying to save the necks of their leaders. They must have been all too aware of the superior forces ranged against them just outside of the town. Whatever the reasons, a deal was struck. The abbey charters were to be given back in return for a promise of no retaliation from the monks. They had reckoned, however, without the royal group itself. Tressilian especially would have no truck with any deal to save the rebels. He swooped on the town and had sixteen of the rebels tried. The jury members were instructed to find the accused guilty. Having been told that the accused would be retried until a guilty verdict had been returned and on pain of being put on trial themselves, the jurors did Tressilian's bidding. On 15 July, Grindecobbe and the other condemned rebels were hanged and drawn.

> *Then they were left swinging, as a warning to other dreamers, on the gibbets for 'as long as they could last' — in other words, until they rotted, stinking, and fell to shreds, until the birds had plucked out their eyes, pecked away whatever flesh was left, until only bones rattled in chains.*[13]

Grindecobbe's supporters could not stand to have their hero displayed with such indignity. At night they cut down Grindecobbe's body and those of the other rebels to give them a proper burial. Tressilian's revenge, however, was not finished:

> *When the authorities saw the fruitless gallows in the morning, they arrested a number of the town's most prominent citizens and forced them to dig up the corpses to hang the rotting vermin-crawling remains once more against the sky.*[14]

Another was executed that day at St Albans. John Ball, the inspiration of the revolt, the priest with indignant anger at the social injustice of his world and a vision of how things might be different, was put to death by the rope and the disembowelling knife. He had been arrested at Coventry and then brought to Tressilian at St Albans on 13 June. Faced with the most gruesome of deaths, he refused to bow to Tressilian's court. He gladly accepted responsibility for his role in the revolt. He said that he had written the letters dispatched to the regions instructing them to rise and that he was right and proud to have done so. He refused to beg for a king's pardon. Tressilian could not break this priest. Ball had been agitating for the vision that drove him for too long to give way now. After twenty years of preaching on village greens and inspiring his followers, he had reached out and fleetingly touched his dream. He had seen men and women who were once cowed under the bailiff's rod throw off their servility and walk on to the stage of history as human beings determined to change their world. No judge would make him flinch.

Ball's death was postponed for two days on the intervention of Bishop Courtenay of London, who had harassed Ball the whole of his politically active life. The authorities wanted more from Ball and in the abbey dungeon they interrogated him. Ball revealed that he had been influenced by some of the ideas of Wycliffe and that the intention of the revolt had been to turn the realm 'upside down' within two years. Now Ball was taken to the place of his execution. He was hanged till nearly dead, then his entrails were drawn and finally his corpse was hacked into four quarters and sent to different regions to be displayed as an example to all those who had shared his dream.

There is something in the grisly nature of Ball's execution that reflects the fear that England's rulers had of what he represented. For them his execution was a cathartic act, a venting of their fear of the masses. Although the revolt was over, they could not erase the fact that it had happened. The peasants, the lowest of the low, had risen and faced their rulers as equals. They had shown that they were neither mere chattel nor mere muscle and brawn. By rising, not just against this or that lord, but rather against feudalism itself, they had shown that they were men and women, human beings who longed with a passion to live differently and to live freely. The villeins of England had not won their freedom this time, but they had changed history – and themselves – forever.

In *The Dream of John Ball*, William Morris imagines himself talking to Ball on the morning of his execution. His words are a fine tribute to the rebels of 1381:

> *John Ball, be of good cheer; for once more thou knowest, as I
> know, that the Fellowship of Man shall endure, however many
> tribulations it may have to wear through . . . it may well be that
> this bright day of summer which is now dawning upon us is no
> image of the beginning of the day that shall be; but rather shall*

that day dawn be cold and grey and surly; and yet by its light shall men see things as they verily are, and, no longer enchanted by the gleam of the moon and the glamour of the dream tide. By such grey light shall wise men and valiant souls see remedy, and deal with it, a real thing that may be touched and handled and no glory of the heavens to be worshipped from afar off. And what shall it be, as I told thee before, save that men shall be determined to be free; yea free as thou wouldst have them, when thine hope rises the highest, and thou art thinking, not of the king's uncles and the poll-groat bailiffs, and the villeinage of Essex, but of the end of it all, when men shall have the fruits of the earth and the fruits of their toil thereon, without money and without price. The time shall come, John Ball, when that dream of thine shall this one day be, shall be a thing that man shall talk of soberly, and as a thing soon to come about, as even with thee they talk of the villeins becoming tenants paying their lord quid-rent; therefore, hast thou done well to hope it . . . and thy name shall abide by thy hope in those days to come, and thou shall not be forgotten.[15]

CHAPTER 6

REFLECTIONS ON THE REVOLT

Like any great event in history, the Peasants' Rising of 1381 has come to represent more than simply the sequence of events that make up the story. It has become a lodestone of political sympathies – for the people or for the state, for freedoms or for restraint, for the worker or for the boss. At decisive moments in British history, the memory of the rebels of 1381 has been invoked and fought over.

The way in which the story has been told has always reflected the political antagonisms of the time. Indeed, this is even true of the early chronicles. The chronicles written during Richard's reign, for example, such as the Anglo-French *Anonimalle Chronicle*, portray him in a heroic light. Similarly, Jean Froissart in his *Chronicles of England, France, Spain and the Adjoining Countries* (1326–1400) is sympathetic to the English king. An exception to this can be found in the pro-Gaunt sentiments of the author of *Knighton's Chronicon*, whose abbey at Leicester had benefited from Gaunt's patronage. The accounts largely written following the Lancastrian inheritance of the crown – in the line of John of Gaunt – after 1399, however, such as those by Thomas Walsingham (the *Historia Anglicana* and the *Ypodigma Neastriae (Demonstrations of Events in Normandy)*) and Thomas Otterbourne's *Chronica Regum Anglæ*, whilst in no way sympathetic to the rebels, portray Richard in a negative and cowardly light.

The general lack of sympathy for the peasants is easy to understand when one considers that many of the chronicles of this era were written by monks at St Alban's Abbey or, as in the case of the *Historia Vitae et Regni Ricardi II* written by the Monk of Evesham, closely followed the accounts given by them.[1] Other accounts written some years after the events of 1381 drew on chronicles written in London. An example is the *Chronicon Westmonasteriense (The Westminster Chronicle)*, which exonerates the London population, portraying the Kentish and Essex armies as a drunken rabble purely intent on destruction.

In the seventeenth century, the more radical elements of Protestantism identified strongly with the revolt. For them it represented a heroic attempt to restore the freedoms of a mythologized pre-Norman England. The Royalist camp, of course, saw the rising differently. When Charles I refused parliamentary rule in 1642, he invoked the memory of the rising as having been a time when the Commons had brought a 'chaos of confusion' upon England. The playwright John Cleveland, in *The Idol of the Clownes* of 1654, depicted the revolt as an early example of the same kind of subversion that was bedevilling the English nation in his own time.[2]

By the eighteenth century, the stories of Wat Tyler, Jack Straw, John Ball and the peasants of Kent and Essex were a part of popular culture. Their memories were celebrated in popular songs and derided in events such as the City of London's 'Annual Triumphal Show'. The revolutionary legacy of the Peasants' Revolt was again debated under the impact of the 1789 revolution in France. Edmund Burke, in his vitriolic condemnation of the revolution, referred to the time of the rising of 1381 as a 'dark age'. In his response to Burke in *The Rights of Man*, Thomas Paine vigorously defended the revolt and its captain:

> *Tyler appears to have been an intrepid, disinterested man, with respect to himself. All his proposals made to Richard, were on a more just and public ground than those which had been made to John by the barons; and not withstanding the sycophancy of the historians, and men like Mr Burke, who seek to gloss over a base action of the court by traducing Tyler, his fame will outlive their falsehood.*[3]

Histories of the rising in the modern era have also reproduced the same polarization of interpretations. The most hostile is that written by Charles Oman, which was published by Oxford University Press in 1906. It would be hard to find a better example of a historian resenting their subject matter in the way Oman does. His comments on Wat Tyler speak volumes:

> *It is probable that he was an adventurer of unknown antecedents, and we may believe the Kentishman who declared that he was a well known rogue and highwayman . . . But*

whatever may have been Tyler's antecedents, we know that he was a quick-witted, self reliant, ambitious fellow, with an insolent tongue, and the gift of magniloquence, which a mob orator needs. That he was anything more than a bold and ready demagogue there is no proof whatever.[4]

For Oman the revolt was a scurrilous affair from start to finish, an episode that should never have occurred. To Oman and historians like him, revolt and revolutions are interruptions in the 'normal' flow of history, irrational outbursts that frustrate the patient work of 'good' men and sometimes even the occasional 'good' woman – a queen perhaps – in the general improvement of society. Oman's argument is that changes in English society, such as the manumissions of the serfs, were already occurring and would have continued without the revolt having happened at all.

A moment's reflection reveals the ahistorical notions behind such approaches to history. It is as though history were a thing in itself, a process that is in some sense independent of what human beings do. But 'history', as Marx said, is nothing. It is the conscious actions of men and women that make history the thing that it is. An episode like the revolt of 1381 may take a long time in coming. Slow cumulative economic and political changes are necessary to produce the conditions that eventually explode in rebellion. Indeed, we have seen the thirty-year period over which frustrations and political resentment built up to produce the revolt. We have seen how the impact of the Black Death produced a demographic crisis in England in the middle of the fourteenth century, and how this put the villeins in a position to bargain with their lords over wages to work demesne land. We have also seen how this coincided with the ideological crisis of the Church, the political crisis in the conflict between the Good Parliament and John of Gaunt, and the strain of war. Finally, we have seen the attempt at a feudal reaction as a section of the ruling elite tried to reassert the power of the fragmenting manorial system, which had held the bailiff's rod over the back of the bondsman. A slow process, yes, but one which finally erupted in the revolt of the villein. Slow, quantitative change eventually becomes sudden, qualitative change. The two are inseparable and together make up the totality of the historical process.

In fact the revolt did play a decisive role in putting an end to villeinage and to the economic basis of feudalism itself. Although there was an initial reaction which was intent on reasserting the power of the manor and which did suppress the peasants for a time, this did not last. The effect of the revolt had been too profound for that. Even the establishment historian G. M. Trevelyan, despite his Whiggish prejudices, acknowledges as much:

> *The demand for freedom, which had been the chief cause of the revolt, was for the moment crushed . . . The Rising had failed . . . But the memory of this terrible year must certainly have acted in another way besides. The landlord had learned to fear his serf, and fear is no less a powerful motive for concession than love. The peasantry were not tamed by the terrors of royal justice. Unions of villains continued to assert their freedom as before.*[5]

The rulers of England had seen what their vassals were capable of. They had stared revolution in the face and they did not like it. The peasants also now saw themselves differently. They had struck hard at the foundations of the feudal order, they had stood before their oppressors as equals and they had negotiated with the king. The relationships and mentalities forming the glue that held society together had changed forever. Also, revolt did not suddenly and completely disappear. Indeed, an attempt at a second rising was made the following year and reports of local revolts and disturbances pepper the history of subsequent decades.

A permanent shift in the national consciousness had occurred. Lords were now more inclined to concede freedom to their villeins when challenged. The number of manumissions granted by the manorial, shire and royal courts increased by the year. Within 50 years villeinage had disappeared from England, at least a century before any other part of Europe.

Another feature of the revolt which was to have profound and lasting consequences was the deep sense of anti-clerical feeling that had been manifested in the attacks on the abbeys and in the execution of Sudbury. The revolt had been permeated with a powerful Christian fundamentalism and a hostility to the wealth and ostentation of Rome. This anti-Papalism was to develop over the next three centuries to find its ultimate expression in the beheading of the Catholic king Charles I. There is a sense in which, in terms of the economic dislocation and the quickening pace of social change and ideological shift, the seventeenth century could not have happened without the fourteenth. When this longer-term and deeper historical significance of the revolt is appreciated, the narrowness of Oman's judgements stands clearly exposed.

In the twentieth century, a handful of excellent histories of the rising were written by historians associated with the Marxist tradition. Hyman Fagan's book, *Nine Days That Shook England*, published in 1938 by the Left Book Club, was associated with the British Communist Party. The Trotskyism of Reg Groves, co-author with Philip Lindsay of *The Peasants' Revolt 1381*, marks that book also as clearly belonging to the lineage of left socialist writings on the events of 1381. What these books share is an unapologetic celebration of the actions of the peasants and an unambiguous identification with their social experience and with their cause. We should include here also the more analytical Marxist writings of Rodney Hilton. In each case the story of the rising has been marshalled to a particular end. In the case of Fagan it was the ideological struggle against the rise of fascism in Europe. In the case of Lindsay and Groves it was about establishing a non-Stalinist tradition of English revolutionary history writing. For Hilton it was about developing the 'history from below' perspectives associated with the British Marxist Historians group and identifying with the radical movements of the 1960s.

We can see, then, that again and again Tyler's revolt has captured the imaginations of historians and has served as a metaphor for feelings, aspirations and antagonisms of the times in which they have written. This has been true despite the vast social and political changes that have occurred from the time of the rebellion to the present day. It is testament to the power of the story of the revolt that it can inspire each generation in ways that resonate with their own social and historical experience.

In 1381 the peasants of England made a leap of consciousness marking the beginning of a wave of revolt that was to sweep eastwards into central Europe. Crucial to this new way of thinking was the idea of freedom. The manorial system had been breaking up for thirty years before the revolt and with it the particular relation between the lord and his serfs. The labour shortage created by plague, the escaping of the serfs and the increasing importance of money and waged labour meant that the individual peasant was no longer beholden to an individual lord. The feudal system was breaking down, though the capitalist system that was to follow had not yet really begun. These changes spelt the end of the old relations of patronage and personal duties and obligations. This in turn created the objective potential for a more generalized consciousness of opposition between wealthy rulers and those 'who are more like us'.

All of this had taken the fetters off the imagination of the peasant. Whereas previously they had been unable to look beyond the boundaries of the manor, now they looked far beyond them. The highest expression of this new consciousness was found in the idealism of John Ball and his closest followers. The radicalism of Ball's vision of freedom and of the new society was breathtaking for the age. This was a vision rooted in the *experience* of class, if not yet in the *theorization* of class that the proletarian politics of a very different period was to make possible. It is best described, perhaps, as a radical Christian democracy and a desire to sweep away the power of the lords, cleanse society of corruption and establish a federation of communes.

It is probably too optimistic to suggest that all or even most of the rebels of 1381 were thinking in quite such terms. We can, perhaps, say that at the highest points of the rebellion – on the morning of Ball's sermon at Blackheath and the taking of London, for example – a sense of the potential for really very radical change must have been a part of the excitement of the events. But for most of the rebels, the point of the rising was the abolition of the power of the manor and a concern with personal and economic liberty. In this issue of personal liberty there was a desire for both the freedom to live as one pleased – to marry as one wished without interference from the lord, for example – and the freedom to hire out one's labour to the highest bidder.

We see here for the first time the beginning of a separation – an alienation – of labourers from their labour power. In bondage there was no distinction between the serf as a person and the serf's ability to do work. The serf was there to do the lord's bidding and to work as the lord dictated. But now, with the rise of wage labour, labour power – the capacity to work – had become a thing apart, a commodity owned by the labourer to be sold on a labour market. Now labourers could see themselves as individuals in a very different sense. Their identity was not one with their ability to work. There was a distinction between the two which made it possible, for the first time in the modern sense, to conceive of personal life with all the inchoate desires for rights and freedoms that went with this.

In all of this we see the double meaning of freedom in history. Freedom is both the absence of necessity and a social relationship. From the moment human societies could produce enough wealth for people to be able to lift their heads and minds beyond the tasks of immediate survival, they had been able to conceive of freedom and leisure. But from that same moment those surpluses had become appropriated and controlled by leisured elites. The first glimmer of the possibility of freedom had become associated with the fact of non-freedom as a result of this social relationship. The desire for freedom was from the outset a political thing.

The peasants had felt the easing of compulsion in their lives as their bargaining position had improved. Now they aspired to freedom in its political aspect. Many were the peasants who had already broken out of the particularity of their relationship with an individual lord. They had a sense of a more general relationship with society. They could, after all, work for any lord. They insisted on a right to their opinion about society and their right to criticize whomsoever they pleased. But in the vision of John Ball this notion of freedom was taken to its most radical conclusion. The lowest peasant was as good as, indeed better than, the highest lord. In Ball's conception of freedom, the relationship is not between the individual peasant and this or that individual lord confined within the manor. It is rather a relationship between the individual and the whole of society and is measured in terms of equality and justice. It was in this sense that the rebels raised the banner of Piers Plowman in 1381.

There are the first notions here, perhaps we should say sentiments, of equality, freedom and justice in their political aspects. Those peasants who had already experienced the economic dislocation of the fourteenth century were also those who were the most receptive to the most radical and inspired ideas of the age. It is no coincidence that Ball found his most enthusiastic support amongst the Kentish rebels where villeinage was already a hated memory. It is also no coincidence that it was mainly the Kentish army that stayed after the granting of the Mile End charters to push the revolution further.

What freedom means, of course, changes from one historical period to the next. The demands and aspirations of social movements and revolutions have a social content that is particular to their time. For the peasants of 1381, freedom meant the right to sell their labour power, the right to sell their surplus and the right to move about without harassment from the sheriff. This was the social content of the demands at Mile End and Smithfield. But we are inspired today by this revolt of more than six centuries ago because of the desire for freedom in a more transhistorical sense. The peasants demanded that their relationship with society be one based on complete equality. It is a desire, often suppressed but sometimes apparent, which spans the whole of human history and which we recognize in ourselves. This is the reason why the peasant revolution of 1381 – really the first revolution – has been important for the revolutionary tradition ever since.

In the end, the rebels of 1381 were not so very different from ourselves. Of course, their social experience was very different. But as human beings they yearned for lives that were radically freer and more equal than the ones they had. They were able to make that leap of imagination from 'things as they are' to 'things as they might be'. They wanted lives of free association and free expression, as do we. In our own age – an age of growing rebellion against exploitation, against injustice and against war – there is a new generation who will find that the voices of the peasants, on that 'bright day of summer', speak to them with an eloquence that they will find exhilarating. To discover that you are not the first is a source of both pride and humility.

It is in this spirit that we should never allow the memory and the stories of Wat Tyler, John Ball and the peasant armies of 1381 to fade.

NOTES

Chapter 1   The Medieval Scene

1. Quoted by J. Mackail, *The Life of William Morris*, Longman, 1907, p. 12.

2. For a fascinating insight into the trials and tribulations of daily life in the medieval village, see R. Hilton, *Class Conflict and the Crisis of Feudalism*, Verso, 1990, pp. 19–40, and also R. Hilton, *Bond Men Made Free*, Routledge, 1993, p. 31.

3. See C. Dyer, *Everyday Life in Medieval England*, Hambledon, 1994, pp. 133–65.

4. C. Coulton, *Social Life in Britain from the Conquest to the Reformation*, Cambridge, 1918, p. 308.

5. Dyer, *Everyday Life in Medieval England*, p. 87.

6. See Coulton, *Social Life in Britain*, pp. 301–6.

7. Hilton, *Bond Men Made Free*, p. 35.

8. For a fuller account of the social divisions of labour and of wealth in the society of this period, see S. Waugh, *England in the Reign of Edward III*, Cambridge, 1991, pp. 25–8.

9. Quoted in B. Wilkinson, *The Later Middle Ages in England*, Longman, 1969, p. 202.

10. C. Coulton, *Medieval Panorama*, Cambridge, 1938, p. 76.

11. Ibid., pp. 76–7.

12. Ibid., p. 123.

13. Quoted by Coulton, *Social Life in Britain*, p. 251.

14. Quoted by Coulton, *Medieval Panorama*, pp. 21–3.

15. Quoted by Waugh, *England in the Reign of Edward III*, p. 24.

16. For a useful description of the impact of trade on the 'borough economy', see C. Platt, *The English Mediaeval Town*, Paladin, 1979, pp. 93–114.

17. In Coventry the town authorities became so exasperated that they turned to sorcery. They hired the services of John of Nottingham, a worker of spells, to fashion wax figures of the local prior and of the king and then to pierce them with the point of a feather.

Chapter 2   The Making of the Revolt

1. Quoted by M. Prestwich, *The Three Edwards: War and State in England 1272–1377*, Weidenfield and Nicolson, 1980, p. 255.

2. Ibid., p. 257.

3. Quoted from a chronicle known as the Brut, by Prestwich, *The Three Edwards*, p. 260.

4. H. Fagan, *Nine Days That Shook England*, Gollancz, 1938, pp. 62–3.

5. Quoted by R. Dobson, *The Peasants' Revolt of 1381*, Macmillan, 1970, p. 64.

6. J. Ramsey, *Genesis of Lancaster*, Vol. 1, Clarendon, 1913, p. 375.

7. Today this antiquated term has a litigious connotation. Here we can assume it to have meant one who was given to complaint regarding their treatment and conditions.

8. Quoted by Helen Jewell in 'Piers Plowman – a poem of crisis', in W. Childs and J. Taylor (eds), *Politics and Crisis in Fourteenth Century England*, Sutton, 1990, p. 67.

9. Dobson, *The Peasants' Revolt of 1381*, p. 76.

10. A. Goodman, *John of Gaunt*, Longman, 1992, p. 400.

11. D. Seward, *The Hundred Years War: The English in France 1337–1453*, Atheneum, 1978, p. 113.

12. Quoted by W. Ormrod, *The Reign of Edward III*, Yale University Press, 1990, p. 36.

13. See the account given by G. Barraclough, *The Medieval Papacy*, Thames and Hudson, 1968, pp. 140–85.

14. G. Trevelyan, *England in the Age of Wycliffe*, Longman, 1915, p. 80.

15. Prestwich, *The Three Edwards*, p. 285.

16. This picture of Ball is given to us by the contemporary chronicler Jean Froissart. Quoted by Trevelyan, *England in the Age of Wycliffe*, p. 197.

Chapter 3   The Revolt Begins

1. C. Oman, *The Great Revolt of 1381*, Oxford, 1906, p. 27.

2. E. Fryde, *The Great Revolt of 1381*, The Historical Association, 1981, p. 15.

3. For an illuminating explanation of the symbolism of these late-fourteenth-century popular verses, see R. Hilton and H. Fagan, *The English Rising of 1381*, Lawrence and Wishart, 1950, pp. 81–9.

4. Quoted by H. Fagan, *Nine Days That Shook England*, Gollancz, 1938, p. 107.

5. This portrayal of events was given by the Elizabethan historian John Stow. Quoted by P. Lindsay and R. Groves, *The Peasants' Revolt 1381*, Hutchinson, 1950, p. 82.

6. This passage can be found in the medieval script known as the *Anonimalle Chronicle*. Quoted by M. Collis, *The Hurling Time*, Faber and Faber, 1958, p. 245.

7. John Shepe is an assumed name. The reference to St Mary's parish of York and to the city of Colchester makes it clear that Ball is referring to himself.

8. Hob the Robber was the popular name for Robert Hales, who had become the king's treasurer six months before the rising. He was a hated figure.

9. This is a reference to Langland's poem, *Piers Plowman*. In the poem Piers

Plowman goes in search of those who are pure in spirit and meets 'Do Well', who protects those who live by their own labour, and 'Do Better', who helps those who are in need.

10. This explanation of what Stow referred to as the 'dark riddles' of these verses is given by R. Hilton and H. Fagan, *The English Rising of 1381*, Lawrence and Wishart, 1950, pp. 100–3.

Chapter 4   The Taking of London

1. It was Bolingbroke who would later overthrow and execute Richard, recently returned from his plunder in Ireland, in a violent coup. This became known as the Revolution of 1399.

2. N. Saul, *Richard II*, Yale University Press, 1997, p. 63.

3. From Stow's translation of the *Chronicon Angliæ* quoted by R. Hilton and H. Fagan, *The English Rising of 1381*, Lawrence and Wishart, 1950, pp. 111–12.

4. Quoted by Hilton and Fagan, *The English Rising of 1381*, p. 113.

5. Quoted by P. Lindsay and R. Groves, *The Peasants' Revolt 1381*, Hutchinson, 1950, p. 102.

6. See the account of these tensions given by R. Webber, *The Peasants' Revolt*, Dalton, 1980, pp. 62–3.

7. The *Anonimalle Chronicle* suggests the probably exaggerated figure of 100,000 peasants in London on 13 June.

8. The Knights of St John had been founded in the twelfth century and had provided hospitals for the treatment of pilgrims who had fallen ill on their journeys to the Holy Land. Along with the Knights Templar, the order had risen to a powerful position in society by virtue of its involvement in the pilgrimages and murderous crusades of that era. The prominence of the Knights was reflected in the fact that their prior, Robert Hales, had been recently appointed as the king's treasurer. Following the suppression of the rising, the Knights had to be forced to return by a royal edict after they had abandoned their uniforms and fled in fear of their lives.

9. Quoted by H. Fagan, *Nine Days That Shook England*, Gollancz, 1938, p. 175.

10. Quoted from Charles Oman's translation of the Anglo-French *Anonimalle Chronicle of St Mary's*, York, in C. Oman, *The Great Revolt of 1381*, Oxford University Press, 1906, p. 195.

11. Quoted by M. Collis, *The Hurling Time*, Faber and Faber, 1958, p. 268.

12. From the *Dictionary of National Biography*, quoted by Fagan, *Nine Days That Shook England*, p. 168.

13. From the *Anonimalle Chronicle*, quoted by Fagan, *Nine Days That Shook England*, p. 189.

14. Quoted from the chronicles by M. McKisack, *The Fourteenth Century 1307–1399*, Oxford, 1988, p. 411.

15. From the *Anonimalle Chronicle of St Mary's*, York, in Oman, *The Great Revolt*, p. 198.

16. 'Total peace': in other words, complete acceptance of this new order. Quoted by Fagan, *Nine Days That Shook England*, p. 195.

17. From the *Anonimalle Chronicle of St Mary's*, York, in Oman, *The Great Revolt*, p. 198.

18. Quoted by Fagan, *Nine Days That Shook England*, p. 227.

19. Lindsay and Groves, *The Peasants' Revolt 1381*, p. 128.

Chapter 5   Repression and Continuing Revolt

1. Mousehold Heath was to serve as the mustering site of another English people's rising when Robert Kett gathered his forces there in 1549.

2. E. Powell, *The Rising in East Anglia in 1381*, Cambridge, 1896, p. 53.

3. C. Oman, *The Great Revolt of 1381*, Oxford University Press, 1906, p. 127.

4. Quoted from the *Chronicon Angliæ* in Oman, *The Great Revolt of 1381*, p. 82.

5. Quoted from Stow's account by H. Fagan, *Nine Days That Shook England*, Gollancz, 1938, p. 252.

6. Quoted in L. Cowie, *The Black Death and the Peasants' Revolt*, Wayland, 1972, p. 114.

7. It is sad to have to note a single exception to this otherwise truly impressive aspect of the revolt. John Wraw, leader of the East Anglian rebellion, turned king's evidence and betrayed his lieutenants. As is so often the case, he did not in so doing earn the respect of his captors and he too went to his death at the hand of William Ufford.

8. Fagan, *Nine Days That Shook England*, p. 256.

9. This story is well told by P. Lindsay and R. Groves, *The Peasants' Revolt 1381*, Hutchinson, 1950. The account given here leans heavily on their narrative.

10. Ibid., p. 144.

11. Quoted ibid., p. 147.

12. Quoted ibid., p. 148.

13. Ibid., p. 149.

14. Ibid., p. 150.

15. W. Morris, *A Dream of John Ball*, Lawrence and Wishart, 1977, pp. 110–11.

Chapter 6   Reflections on the Revolt

1. For an authoritative account of the political motives behind the early chronicles, see L. Duls, *Richard II in the Early Chronicles*, Mouton, 1975.

2. See the fascinating account of the political use of the legacy of the rising in the seventeenth and eighteenth centuries given by A. Dunn, *The Great Rising of 1381*, Tempus, 2002, pp. 149–52.

3. Quoted ibid., p. 151.

4. C. Oman, *The Great Revolt of 1381*, Oxford University Press, 1906, pp. 36–7.

5. G. Trevelyan, *England in the Age of Wycliffe*, Longman, 1915, p. 254.

INDEX